OWN YOUR MOMENTUM

Silence Self-Doubt, Break Limiting Patterns, and Step into Success

JEREMY JOHNSON

Story **BUILDERS** P R E S S

To my three sons, Cameron, Gavin, and Mason

And to every person who refuses an average life and chooses to build a life on purpose. Your choices matter more than your circumstances.

CONTENTS

INTRODUCTION

efore you dive in, there's one thing I want you to know. My intention is that you read this book with a pen or pencil in hand. I really mean that. This book isn't meant for you to read once, shrug, and say, "Well, that was good" as you stick it on your shelf and forget about it. My hope is that you come back to these pages over and over, and that every time you do, something different stands out. That's the cool thing about continuous growth. The next time you read this, you won't be the same person you are right now. And different things I've said will hit differently for you based on where you are then.

This may sound a little spiritual, but it's the best way I can explain what I mean. When you read the Bible or any scripture, you take something completely different from it depending on what season of life you're in. What you read today won't be something you'll want to highlight ten years from now. What you're going through, what you're learning, and what you're wrestling with will change how the words land on your heart. Your momentum will be different every year, so the way these ideas reach you will evolve right along with you.

The words on these pages matter, but what you hear inside yourself as you read them matters even more. If you feel a nudge or get a flash of inspiration or clarity, write it down before it slips away. Don't trust yourself to remember it later. Some of the most important ideas you'll get

Your momentum will be different every year, so the way these ideas reach you will evolve right along with you.

while going through this book won't come from me at all. They'll come from your own thoughts, your own soul or inner wisdom, or whatever you want to call it. My words are just a conduit.

They're simply here to open the door for whatever your mind wants to show you about where you're going, what matters most to you, and what needs to change.

That's why I want this book to be something you return to, not just something you finish. Pay attention to what stands out. Highlight it. Write notes in the margins. Record the thoughts that come to you while you're reading. Those thoughts will tell you what momentum looks like for you, what fulfillment means to you, what choices you need to make, and what needs to shift in your life.

By the time you reach the end of this book, my hope is that you feel excited about your progress toward the person you're becoming. I want you to feel the possibilities in front of you. You have the opportunity to be the best version of yourself today, and even better tomorrow.

I've read many books over the years, and I don't think any of those authors told me, "Hey, come back to this every year. I want this to be a manual for your growth." But that's exactly what I want for you. This is a "pick it up once a year" kind of book. And every time you do, you'll meet a new version of yourself on these same pages. Let's do this.

CHAPTER 1

A WONDERFUL LIFE?

For more than twenty years, I've had this relentless dream: *I'm going to write a book.* Some days it felt like a fleeting whisper, barely noticeable. Others, it hit me right between the eyes. Hard.

During a recent decluttering experience, I came across an old journal. The first entry I flipped to was dated October 21, 2001. Back then I lived in Provo, Utah, and had just graduated from Brigham Young University. It read:

> *My whole goal in life is to find something I love doing and to be able to influence people for good. If that means church service, writing a book on self-discipline, or owning a company, I will do it. . . . I hope I am ready to see and take the opportunity when it comes my way.*

The irony isn't lost on me.

Here I am, the author of a book on momentum. I finally got serious about writing almost a quarter of a century after I said I wanted to do it.

So what changed? And why now?

Sure, there was some dabbling and note-taking, some days of deep thinking and reflection. But that's where it ended. I'd hear a podcast or listen to an audiobook and think, *Man, this is such a good book. I'd love to share my story and experiences and help somebody else.* I'd grab the nearest notebook and go to town writing the life stories I thought could inspire someone else to get up and do the thing that was on their heart. Then the doubts would come creeping in, *Why me? I'm not a psychologist. I don't know how to write a book. I have no clue how to format it or cite sources I want to use. Who cares what I have to say anyway?*

A few days would pass, and then a new thought would come. More insights would show up, and I'd have more to write down. The cycle continued.

I need to do this.

I can't.

Oh, that was so inspiring. I know what I have to say can help others.

I really *need to do this. I can't . . .*

Like many other people, I knew what I wanted to do, but I always came up with reasons that kept me from moving forward.

Things started to accelerate, and my mindset began to shift when I attended Brendon Burchard's influencer seminar. When he talked about being vulnerable and telling your story, it hit me again: *I need to write my book.* Recently, I attended a two-day conference, the Summit of Greatness, in Los Angeles with Lewis Howes and his guests. One of the speakers owns a company that helps people write books, and he talked about that during the lunch hour session. His question—*Why not now?*—seemed to be directed right at me, so before I could change my mind, I signed up to meet with someone on his team before the end of the conference to see how to get started. Unfortunately, my time slot for that meeting was based on the wrong time zone, and I had to leave to catch my flight, so it didn't happen then. It made me wonder if that was a sign not to write.

Shortly afterward, while I was doing some business planning for the new year, I watched a goal-setting workshop led by Jon Acuff on my computer at home. He looked directly into my eyes through the camera and said, "You're gonna write your book this year. This is your year."

That's when I knew beyond a shadow of a doubt that it was time to start. So I contacted that book-writing company, made a new appointment, and got to work.

And here I am today, excited to share what I've learned and to help you obtain, regain, and sustain the momentum you need to follow the relentless dream on *your* heart that just won't leave you alone. Let's get started.

INTERPRET YOUR INHIBITORS

Maybe you've noticed that you feel excited to get moving on your dream. You do a little future casting and visualize yourself after you've done the thing. Smiling to yourself, you start thinking, *This is it. I'm really going to do it this time.*

You get started. You see yourself making progress, and it's incredible.

But then you hit a wall after a few weeks and wonder how your dream has come to a screeching halt once more.

When we lose momentum, it can cause mental fatigue—we *know* we can do better, but we feel like we're at a loss. We struggle with the tension between where we are and where we want to be. We question our character and integrity when we aren't living up to our ambitions. We feel the weight of regret and want to feel better.

But what if we took the time to see those interruptions for what they are, made adjustments, and got back on track instead of gaining momentum in a negative downward spiral? In the next chapter, we'll go deeper into the reasons we lose our momentum, but for now, let's look at three big inhibitors that I've found: worry, shame, and distractions.

We all worry. Some of us are just better at hiding it than others. Worry manifests itself in different forms for each of us. Instead of motivating us, it tends to paralyze us into a state of inaction. One day leads to the next, and our dreams keep floating in and out of our lives without getting any closer to becoming a reality.

In his book *How to Stop Worrying and Start Living: Time-Tested Methods for Conquering Worry,* Dale Carnegie writes, "One of the most tragic things I know about human nature is that all of us tend to put off living. We are all dreaming of some magical rose garden over the horizon instead of enjoying the roses that are blooming outside our windows today. Why are we such fools—such tragic fools?"[1]

In the early years of my career, I spent too much time worrying about how I was going to provide for my family. I don't want you to make the same mistake and worry your life away. There isn't anything wrong with acknowledging our fears—it's much healthier than trying to ignore them. But we can't let our fears keep us from moving forward. Worry robs us of the choice to focus on the present moment and instead keeps us dwelling on the past or fearing the future. What controls your thoughts controls your attention. And in turn, what controls your attention controls your life. Would you rather aim your attention to what is positive and hopeful, or negative and worrisome?

Of course, if you feel like anxiety is interfering with your ability to perform normal everyday tasks, there is nothing wrong with talking to a mental health professional to create a path toward healing. But if it's just an unfounded, nagging worry, it can be a momentum-killer that you must deal with now.

Shame is one of the biggest inhibitors of momentum. It keeps us stuck, convincing us that we've already failed too many times to try again. Shame tells us that our past missteps define us, making us hesitant to take risks or commit to something new.

But that's a lie.

The truth is, everyone stumbles. Everyone has moments of uncertainty. What separates those who build momentum from those who stay stuck is the ability to let go of shame and move forward anyway. Brené Brown said it best: "Shame corrodes the very part of us that believes we are capable of change."[2]

> **What controls your attention controls your life.**

You are capable of making a change to create your momentum and see your relentless dream come to fruition. You are worthy of making progress and succeeding. No past failure can keep you from the success you're meant for—unless you let it.

You may be surprised to learn that technology isn't the problem. The overabundance of distractions isn't the problem either. It's the *overconsumption* of the technology available to us that derails our momentum. There is an opportunity cost of time lost when we overconsume technology (social media, streaming services, gaming). Giving in to these distractions can become addictive over time.

How many times has a streaming service asked if you're still watching a program because you've been inactive for so long? Now, be honest. How many times have you chosen, "Don't ask again" as you roll your eyes at the screen for asking you such a question?

What would happen if we could take the time we spend watching "just one more episode" and use it to move a little closer to a relentless dream?

Our human tendency is to crave immediate gratification. Why is that? It's biological. The adrenal gland in our brain releases the hormone dopamine, which strongly favors immediate rewards over delayed ones because historically, quick payoffs meant survival. These instant decisions require less cognitive effort than delayed planning. And preferring immediate gratification conserves mental energy. In short, wanting instant gratification is not a moral failure. It is a deeply rooted survival adaptation. But self-control requires actively overriding ancient biological wiring. So if we want to gain momentum, we must forego immediate gratification to gain lasting success by achieving our goals. We are worth so much more than simply making it to the next episode, level, or post to like.

What relentless dream tugs at you even now? And how would it feel to see it in your reality? Maybe you signed up for an online course and only got through the first three modules before you lost interest. Maybe you walk past the guitar hanging on your wall as it collects dust, thinking that tomorrow will be a great day to start strumming it again. Maybe it's a song you put so much effort into but ended up shelving it before you finished.

You might have told yourself that your dream is something from your childhood that doesn't belong in your grown-up life. Maybe you think you're too old to learn a new instrument or take up a new hobby you've never tried before.

We let go of dreams all the time. We have goals that light a fire in our hearts, but then something turns that flame into a flicker or just a little stream of smoke. We say things like "Life got in the way." Our priorities shift, and responsibilities pile up. Doubt creeps in, and somewhere along the way, we let it go.

Maybe you've even convinced yourself that your dream wasn't that important to begin with. But deep down, it's still there. You can feel it—the weight of what could have been, the quiet disappointment of not seeing it through.

> **We have goals that light a fire in our hearts, but then something turns that flame into a flicker or just a little stream of smoke.**

If that sounds familiar, hear this: You are not alone. Many of us have let go of our dreams because we got busy, discouraged, or talked ourselves out of them because we weren't sure where to start or how to get help. Sometimes we let go because we're afraid of failing, of what people will think, or that we're not as talented or strong as we had hoped.

Here's the truth: Dreams don't expire. Your potential doesn't have an expiration date either. If you still have moments when you have that relentless dream, then it's not too late.

WHERE MOMENTUM AND HUMAN POTENTIAL COLLIDE

Every holiday season, I have to watch *It's a Wonderful Life*. And when I do, I can't *not* get emotional—not just because it's a great story but because it contains elements of my own story. If you've ever found yourself at rock bottom, you know what I mean.

In 2006, I cofounded a title company and was originating mortgage loans. Needless to say, starting a title company when the real estate market was starting to take a nosedive during the American subprime mortgage crisis was not a good idea. During that time, I had to pay an overdraft fee to my bank after buying my son a McDonald's Happy Meal even though I knew we didn't have that much money in our account. That was my George Bailey moment when I started questioning what I was doing with my life.

> **If you still have moments when you have that relentless dream, then it's not too late.**

In the movie, George has big dreams. He wants to travel and build great things, but life has other plans. He stays home, runs his family's savings and loan business, and watches others live the life he once imagined. When everything starts to collapse and he thinks he's failed everyone—and even more critically, himself—he starts to believe the world might be better off without him.

I know that feeling. Maybe you do too. There were many times I wondered whether my life insurance policy was worth more than I was. Your confidence wavers, and even though you know what to do to get unstuck, fear and hopelessness paralyze you. They make you feel like momentum has come to a dead stop. But here's the thing: Momentum is always there, even when we can't see it.

Like George, I had angels around me. They didn't have wings or ring bells, but they were there—friends, family members, and people who reminded me that my story wasn't over. Sometimes, the only thing that keeps us going is the people who lovingly refuse to let us stop.

> **Momentum is always there, even when we can't see it.**

That's the real power of momentum. It's not just about moving forward when things are great. It's about realizing that even in your worst moments, your life still matters. If George had never been born, Bedford Falls would have fallen apart. Families would have lost their homes. His brother wouldn't have been there to save the sailors. Our words and actions (or even inactions) influence others. Every choice we make moves outward beyond us to influence others and situations in ways we may never fully see. To be human is to be an ongoing source of influence, creating ripples simply by existing and acting within our environments.

The same is true for you. You may not realize it, but your presence creates ripples. Every time you show up and push through, even when it's hard, you build momentum. It's not always about giant leaps. Sometimes it's just about making it through the day. Other times, it's about letting others lift you up when you can't do it alone.

The beauty of *It's a Wonderful Life* isn't just that George realizes his worth. It's that the entire town shows up for him. When you live a life of generosity and kindness, people remember. They don't let you fall. They rally. They remind you why you matter.

If you're in a George Bailey moment right now—if you're wondering if anything you do really matters—let me tell you, it does. Your life has weight. Your presence changes things. Momentum isn't just about where you're going; it's about the impact you already make, even if you can't see it yet.

When I was studying psychology at Brigham Young University, I always wondered what made some people seem to have everything so put together while others struggled. Why were some people so happy while others saw life through a negative lens? People striving to do their best stand out from those who don't.

You may not realize it, but your presence creates ripples.

I've always been fascinated by human potential. I believe we aren't meant for mediocrity. We are spiritual beings having a human experience, and with that comes an incredible opportunity to rise above, to overcome, and to become. Yet so many of us live beneath our potential. Why? Because we leave too much to chance. We wake up and react to life rather than intentionally designing it. But here's the truth: Momentum is what separates those who are just getting by from those who are thriving.

Momentum isn't just about going fast or working hard; it's about being intentional, creating systems, and developing habits that push us forward. I chose to study the mind and behavior because I have always been drawn to figuring out why people do what they do, why they make the choices they make, and why they're influenced the way they are. I believe we all have potential—a divine potential, really. I have always wanted to make my life better through personal development so I can make someone else's life better by sharing my knowledge and experience.

Success compounds. But just as quickly, we can lose it altogether.

I learned this firsthand in my career as a mortgage originator. When I first started, I knew that my income was 100 percent commission-based, meaning if I didn't create momentum in my business, I didn't get paid. I couldn't afford to hope things would work out. I had to be intentional. I needed a daily success plan, a routine that would generate results. The roller coaster of one good month followed by a bad month wasn't an option; I had to make my business predictable. That required discipline, consistency, and focus on the highest-impact activities—the ones that actually moved the needle.

It's the same in life. If we aren't intentional about where we want to go, we'll end up wherever the current takes us.

That's not success.

That's drifting.

Drifting often happens quietly when days pass without clear direction and effort becomes reactive instead of intentional. Over time, this lack of focus slows momentum and pulls us off course. We must pivot often. Pivoting is when you pause, reassess, and deliberately change direction. It doesn't require a dramatic overhaul, just a clear decision and a small, intentional step forward. By pivoting, momentum can be rebuilt, and progress resumes with purpose instead of drifting.

The key to pivoting to maintain your momentum is having a powerful *why* that keeps you moving forward even when things get hard. Life happens. Markets crash. Unexpected obstacles pop up. And sometimes, we are the ones who derail our own momentum through poor choices or a lack of discipline. When you keep in mind a clear vision of the life you want to create, it's easier to keep pushing forward.

I've spent years studying success—not just in business but in life. One thing I know for sure is that people who have momentum exude **Momentum is what separates those who are just getting by from those who are thriving.** confidence. They have an energy about them. You can see it in their eyes, their posture, and even the way they carry themselves. They aren't just going through the motions. They're moving toward something meaningful.

That kind of energy is contagious.

I want to help you build momentum in your own life. I believe that you have it in you to do more, be more, and live a life free of regret. The Pareto Principle tells us that 80 percent of our results come from 20 percent of our efforts. That means success isn't about doing everything; it's about doing the right things over and over again.

WHAT IS MOMENTUM?

If you have a goal, there comes a time when you have to start moving toward it. It sounds simple, doesn't it?

However, many people who start their year excited about a New Year's resolution let go of it less than two weeks later. This is such a common phenomenon in the United States that January 19 has been dubbed Quitter's Day.

Why do so many of us find ourselves unable to get started? Or once we do, why can't we follow through and make it successfully to the finish line? Our problem isn't a lack of desire or potential—it's a lack of momentum.

Scientifically, momentum is mass multiplied by velocity. If something takes up a lot of space or is moving quickly, it will take more external force to slow it down or stop it. I've heard people talk about momentum using the analogy of a freight train—it takes a lot of effort and energy to get it going, but once it's in motion, it's unstoppable.

For our purposes, consider the following definition of momentum: "taking consistent action over time." Momentum is not linear for us as human beings. Working quickly won't guarantee constant momentum in your life, nor will taking up all your available time while pushing yourself to focus solely on your goal. Instead, momentum is built through intention, persistence, and the willingness to keep moving forward—even when your progress feels small.

Why does momentum matter? Because it has the power to change everything. Abraham Lincoln is believed to have said that the best way to predict the future is to create it. When you create momentum in your life, you break free from the gravitational pull of hesitation, doubt, and fear. The hardest part is always the beginning—the moment right before you take your first step. Once you do, each step that follows becomes easier, and before you know it, you've built a rhythm. Action breeds more action, and soon, what once might have seemed impossible becomes second nature.

Momentum fuels confidence. When you see yourself making progress, even in small ways, it reinforces your belief that you are capable. When you believe in yourself, you show up differently. You take risks. You make bold moves. You push through challenges instead of backing away from them. You start to realize that success isn't reserved for other people; it's available for you too.

Momentum also creates resilience. Life is full of obstacles, and without them, those challenges can feel like walls that are too high to climb. But when you've built momentum, setbacks don't stop you; they just slow you down temporarily. You've already built the habit of moving forward, so don't let discouragement keep you down. You get back up and keep going more easily.

We are wired for progress. I believe we are children of our Heavenly Father, and with that heritage, we are meant for greatness rather than mediocrity. One of our main objectives in this life is to become who we are meant to be. For each of us, it will look different, but we can't leave it up to chance or randomness. We must have a vision and a reason that is so powerful that it drives us to reach our potential.

The key to transformation isn't a secret formula; it's momentum. Small, consistent actions taken over time lead to exponential growth. If you're waiting for the chance to create your momentum, here it is. Start where you are, take one step, and then another. Your momentum will carry you to places you never imagined possible.

LET'S GET MOVING

What does success look like for you? Maybe it's finally committing to that goal you've been putting off. Maybe it's creating a daily routine that helps you start each day with positive intentions. Maybe it's eliminating distractions and focusing only on what truly matters to you. Whatever it is, you already know deep down what you need to do. The only real question is this: *When will you do it?*

Jim Rohn once said at one of his seminars, "We must all suffer from one of two pains: the pain of discipline or the pain of regret. The difference is discipline weighs ounces while regret weighs tons." I don't want to look back on my life and wonder what could have been. I want to know I gave it my all. And I want the same for you. The great thing is we have freedom of choice. We can choose to be disciplined so we don't end up at the end of our lives with regret.

There is a time and a place for everything we do. Would I have written this book if I had started it the day after my journal entry? Probably not. And that's okay. Looking back on my twenty-two-year-old self, I'd tell him not to beat himself up over not writing the book. I'd encourage him by letting him know that his wife and kids will soon be his number-one priority, and that through life experience, learning, and growing, he'll make it happen later. Have I wanted to write a book all along? Sure. But I don't know in my heart of hearts that I would have been able to do it the way I wanted to back then as a recent college graduate.

This isn't about looking at what you didn't do yet and telling yourself that you really messed up or that you waited too long to get started. Sometimes it takes time for your circumstances to line up. You find yourself in a place where you have the time and the mental capacity to address the seeds you planted in the past.

Fear of regret can be a powerful motivator. None of us knows how much time we have, but we do know this: Time will pass whether we take action or not. I'd rather spend my time building something meaningful, wouldn't you?

It all starts with creating momentum.

Momentum begins with knowledge. Depending on the direction you wish to go, you must study and learn. You have to develop skills. Once you have the knowledge and skills, you can set clear goals and a vision of where you want to go.

What good is momentum if you don't know the direction you want to go?

An airplane rarely flies in a perfectly straight line to its destination. Wind, weather, and small deviations constantly push it off course, often without anyone noticing. What allows the plane to arrive where it's supposed to is not flawless direction but continuous course correction. In the same way, personal progress involves drifting slightly as life applies pressure and distractions. Success isn't about never drifting; it is about noticing early and making small, steady adjustments that keep you moving toward where you want to end up.

We are wired for progress.

Your potential is greater than you think.

You are more capable of achieving your relentless dream than you realize. But you have to take ownership of your momentum. You have to be intentional. You have to decide that you are worth the effort. And you have to have systems in place as you move through the ebb and flow of your life.

It's time to get serious about your next step.

THE STRUGGLE OF BEING STUCK

I remember exactly what it felt like to be stuck. Not just stuck in the way we sometimes feel after one bad day, but deeply, frustratingly stuck—like wading through knee-deep mud with no clear path forward.

When I graduated from college, I felt completely unsure of what was next. I grew up watching my dad build a successful career in commercial real estate. He had reached a point early in life where he worked because he wanted to, not because he had to. My siblings and I were his landscaping crew growing up, and while I resented it at the time, I now see the gift in that experience. Not only did we learn the value of hard work, but we also grew closer as siblings because we were going through it together.

My dad's life showed me the power of being your own boss, having your income tied to your efforts, and creating a life where work didn't control you. That idea stuck with me. I wanted to make a difference, but what did that even look like? With a degree in psychology and my interest in human potential, I knew that to go further in the field, I'd need an advanced degree. My plan was to pursue a Master's in Organizational Behavior, but life had other ideas.

At the time, I was working at Executive Excellence, a book publisher focused on excellence. I was surrounded by great minds—people like Ken Shelton who wrote extensively about high achievement, and Douglas Warren, a Total Quality Management consultant who wrote *Mind Over Time*. I was even a teacher's assistant for my psychology professor, Dr. Kenneth Higbee, focusing on memory research and memory tools. I was absorbing all of this, but I still wasn't sure where I fit in.

When I got married, I wanted to find a job that tied my income to my efforts instead of an hourly wage. Real estate kept pulling at me, and I met two successful loan officers who introduced me to the mortgage business. The idea of helping people buy homes—the places where they would create their most treasured memories—resonated with me. The potential for financial freedom and control over my own success was appealing too. So I jumped in.

After my wife graduated from college, we moved to Virginia to be close to her family, and I found a local mortgage company in Northern Virginia that was hiring.

Twenty-five years later, I'm still a mortgage loan originator. Since I started, though, my role has taken on a deeper meaning, knowing I am managing emotions and expectations for people making one of the biggest financial decisions of their lives.

But even with all that, I've had my doubts. Many times along the way, I've asked myself, *Is this the right path?* Looking back now, I believe it was, but that doesn't mean it was easy. There were times I felt stuck, and in those moments, the biggest lesson I learned was this: *Just take action.*

Perfection kills momentum. Waiting for the perfect conditions, the perfect plan, the perfect moment—that's how people stay stuck. Every day I have to remind myself to be intentional about my time and to focus on what moves me closer to my goals.

Momentum is the cure for worry and fear. Taking action, even small steps, creates movement, and movement breaks the feeling of stagnation.

I've also learned that having the right people around you makes all the difference. A coach, a mentor—someone who has walked your path before—can give you the perspective you need to shift from inaction to action.

Life doesn't wait for us to feel ready. The conditions will never be perfect. Whether you're chasing a dream or outrunning fear, the key is movement. Bold action—not just bold thinking—is what creates change. So why is it so hard to go from stuck to moving again?

WHY DO WE STAY STUCK?

Have you ever felt like you're living the same day over and over, watching time slip away while the life you truly want feels just out of reach? Maybe you've told yourself you'll make a change "someday," but someday keeps getting pushed farther into the future. The weight of regret doesn't come all at once—it builds slowly, in quiet moments when you wonder what could have been if only you'd taken that chance, spoken up, or believed in yourself enough to do the thing.

One of the biggest regrets people have when they stay stuck too long is the haunting thought of what might have been. I know this feeling well. There's also the regret of not living up to your full potential, of knowing that time—the greatest gift we have—was not used to its fullest. We all have unique talents and abilities, given to us for a reason, and failing to use them can feel like a deep personal loss. It's not just about career choices or big decisions; sometimes it's the smaller ways we hold back—staying quiet when we want to say something, hesitating when we should take action.

> **Stagnation isn't real. We are always moving, either forward or backward.**

Too often, people sabotage their own momentum by dwelling on past failures. I once heard an analogy that stuck with me: The rearview mirror in a car is small for a reason. It's meant for quick glances to remind us where we've been. But the windshield is large. Where we're going matters so much more. How often do we find ourselves staring backward, replaying mistakes, letting them define what we believe is possible for our lives? I've caught myself doing this, allowing past failures to cast a shadow over my confidence. Imposter syndrome sneaks in, whispering that I'm not good enough or that my past missteps are the whole book, not just part of the story. The future is a blank page, and we get to decide what comes next.

Fear can paralyze us, as Orison Swett Marden describes in his book *The Paralysis of Fear*. He explains that if left unchecked, fear immobilizes us and keeps us from success. But rather than eliminating fear, we need to learn how to harness it. Instead of letting it hinder us, we can use it as a driving force to propel us forward.[3]

> **Perfection kills momentum. Waiting for the perfect conditions, the perfect plan, the perfect moment—that's how people stay stuck.**

I love the analogy of the lion and the gazelle. Every morning in Africa, a gazelle wakes up. It knows it must run faster than the fastest lion or it will be killed. Every morning, a lion wakes up. It knows it must run faster than the slowest gazelle or it will starve. It doesn't matter whether you are the lion or the gazelle—when the sun comes up, you'd better be running.

That's momentum. That's life. You move, or you fall behind.

In his book *Soundtracks,* Jon Acuff shares how the stories we tell ourselves shape our reality, for better or worse. If we repeat negative thoughts, they hold us back. But if we intentionally replace them with positive, action-oriented beliefs, we create momentum instead of fear-driven paralysis.[4]

It's easy to believe that life is stacked against us and that external circumstances keep us from moving forward. And sometimes, real challenges do stand in the way. But the hardest truth—and the most freeing one—is this: Stagnation isn't real. We are always moving, either forward or backward. If we're not building momentum, we're losing it. That's why taking action, even the smallest step, is so critical. Because every step forward, no matter how small, is proof that we are not stuck. We are in motion. And motion is what leads to change.

LESSONS LEARNED

On a recent long flight, I watched *The Natural,* one of my favorite movies. It struck a chord because sports shaped the first twenty years of my life. My dad pushed us hard—too hard I thought back then—but now I understand. He wanted us to be our best, and discipline was his way of ensuring that.

Miss a tackle in football? Keep the pads on and practice at home. Strike out in baseball? Run five laps around the block. Let a ball pass by me as a catcher? My dad would throw balls in the dirt while I blocked them, hands behind my back. Basketball meant dribbling around the block with one hand and then switching to the other. The training was relentless, but it instilled resilience.

At a youth football tournament in Plano, Texas, Heisman Trophy winner Herschel Walker and some Dallas Cowboys shared their training routines. Walker described dragging a car tire with his coach sitting on it to build leg strength. Inspired, my dad had us hauling weights up and down a ditch. Sports were more than a game; they were a proving ground for discipline and perseverance.

That's why *The Natural* resonates so deeply. Roy Hobbs, played by Robert

> **The rearview mirror in a car is small for a reason.**

Redford, was a gifted pitcher whose career was derailed after a tragic shooting. His momentum stopped. He fell into depression and regret, stepping away from the game he loved. But when a second chance came, he seized it. Switching his focus to hitting, he fought his way back, proving himself with action rather than excuses.

Life throws roadblocks at us—some self-inflicted, some beyond our control. But it's our choices, not our circumstances, that define us. Like Roy Hobbs, we can let setbacks paralyze us or use them as fuel to move forward. Every day is a chance to rewrite our story, not dwell on what could have been.

I do believe that regret can be a powerful motivator, as shown in another favorite film, *The Straight Story*. Be forewarned, if you do decide to watch it, make sure you're in the mood for something a little slower than you're used to. It follows Alvin Straight, a seventy-three-year-old veteran who drives a riding lawnmower 240 miles to reconcile with his estranged brother. Unable to drive a car because he couldn't get a driver's license due to his poor eyesight and health conditions, he embarks on this unusual journey, determined to make things right before it's too late.

Life throws roadblocks at us—some self-inflicted, some beyond our control. But it's our choices, not our circumstances, that define us.

Alvin's trip is about more than distance; it's about facing regret head-on. Along the way, he meets people who remind him that everyone carries some burden of remorse. His silent, tear-filled reunion with his brother speaks volumes: While we can't change the past, we can choose to act before regret becomes unbearable.

The key lesson? Acknowledging regret is only the first step; action is what transforms our what-ifs. The difference between a life weighed down by what-ifs and one fueled by momentum is simply the decision to move forward.

HOW DO YOU BREAK FREE?

Feeling stuck can be frustrating, exhausting, and even disheartening. You want to move forward, but you're unable to take the first step. Maybe you feel overwhelmed by choices, paralyzed by fear, or weighed down by past mistakes. Whatever the reason, being stuck isn't just about external circumstances.

Often, when we feel stuck, we seek comfort and distraction. This can look like scrolling, overeating, binge-watching, procrastinating, or even staying busy with low-risk tasks. These behaviors provide short-term relief by calming stress and activating internal reward systems. Sometimes we will even respond to being stuck by clinging tighter to what is familiar, even if it is no longer serving us. Routine feels safe, and changing direction requires energy, vulnerability, and risk—which our brains naturally resist. In short, when we feel stuck, we tend to prioritize emotional relief over long-term progress. But these behaviors keep us stuck.

If you're ready to break free, the first step is to identify what is holding you back. In Chapter 5, we'll explore the deeper causes of stuckness—fear, addiction, negative thought patterns, and emotional paralysis, to name a few. But for now, ask yourself: *Where am I stuck? Where do I see signs of losing momentum in my life?*

One big trap that keeps people stuck is believing that progress needs to be dramatic or instant. But remember, real momentum comes from small, consistent steps. Many people stay paralyzed because they focus too much on the gap between where they are and where they want to be. Instead of letting that distance overwhelm you, shift your focus to what you can do right now.

Your thoughts play a crucial role in whether you stay stuck or move forward. Studies show that 95 percent of our thoughts are the same ones we had the day before. That means if you were filled with self-doubt and hesitation yesterday, it's not going to suddenly change today—unless you make a conscious effort to break the pattern.

Another common misconception about getting unstuck is that you need to feel motivated first. Here's the truth: Motivation is unreliable. It comes and goes, and if you wait for it, you'll stay stuck. Instead, focus on discipline—creating those lasting habits that can keep you going even when you don't feel like it.

Set a non-negotiable daily action, even if it's just ten minutes of focused work or one small step toward your goal. If you struggle with hesitation, try Mel Robbins' five-second rule: If you have an instinct to act, count down from five and do it before your mind can talk you out of it. Tracking your progress can also help. Small wins create motivation over time, and seeing the actions you've taken, even minor ones, builds momentum.

You may think you need to feel ready before you can move forward. But readiness is a myth. You won't suddenly wake up one day with a complete absence of doubt, uncertainty, or fear. Action creates readiness, not the other way around. If you're hesitating, lower the stakes.

Instead of thinking about getting it right or having perfect execution, decide to just take the next manageable step. Breaking tasks into smaller pieces also helps. If something feels overwhelming, slice it into tiny steps. Want to write a book? Start with one sentence. Want to switch careers? Research one company today. Allow yourself to start messy. Progress beats perfection every time.

Having the right support system can make all the difference. Surrounding yourself with people who encourage progress can help you stay on track. Find an accountability partner—someone who will check in on your progress and encourage you when you feel stuck. Join a community, whether it's an online group, a mastermind, or even a mentor or coach. Being around others who are also taking action can keep you inspired.

Allow yourself to start messy. Progress beats perfection every time.

Concurrently, limit time spent with people who reinforce stuckness. If certain relationships drain you or keep you in a negative mindset, it's okay to create some boundaries. Protect your momentum.

The feeling of being stuck doesn't disappear overnight. Every action, no matter how small, creates momentum. Over time, those small actions add up, and suddenly, you're not stuck anymore—you're an object in motion. Instead of focusing on how far you have to go, focus on the next step. Action leads to clarity. Clarity leads to confidence. Confidence leads to more action. And before you know it, you're no longer standing still—you're moving forward.

So where can you start today? One small step is all it takes to begin to break free.

BUILD YOUR MOMENTUM

Feeling stuck is one of the most frustrating experiences in life. It can make even the simplest tasks feel impossible and rob us of our sense of purpose. But here's the good news: You don't have to stay stuck. Small, intentional actions can help you build momentum, break through feelings of stagnation, and move forward with confidence. Here's how you can begin your journey today.

Start your day with purpose. One of the simplest yet most effective ways to break free from feeling stuck is to start your day with intention. No, I don't mean immediately jumping into work emails or social media. Instead, use your mornings to set the tone for the day. As Jim Rohn says, "Never begin your day until it is finished on paper." Action without direction rarely leads to progress and momentum.

In my life, I begin with prayer. I once heard that your knees should be the first thing to hit the ground in the morning, not your feet. And that idea has stuck with me. Then, once I'm awake and ready to start the day, I listen to *The Daily Fire* from the GrowthDay app by Brendon Burchard.

Instead of reacting to the world first thing in the morning, create a space for yourself. Rita Mae Brown once said, "A life of reaction is a life of slavery, intellectually and spiritually. One must fight for a life of action, not reaction." Some of the best morning practices include prayer or meditation, reading something inspiring, writing down your thoughts or intentions, exercising or moving, hydrating, practicing deep breathing exercises, reading your favorite affirmations, and listening to uplifting music or positive content.

Music has a profound impact on your mindset. If you doubt its power, I highly recommend Don Campbell's book *The Mozart Effect*, which explores how music can heal, strengthen the mind, and unlock creativity.

Beginning your day with actions that fuel you sets you up for a positive and productive mindset. The most important part of your morning is to set the tone for your day.

Reframe limiting beliefs. When facing challenges, I used to wonder, *Why me?* But then I shifted it to, *Why not me?* The difference between those two questions is everything. Here's the truth: Ordinary people do extraordinary things all the time. If they can, why can't you?

Some common limiting beliefs that keep people stuck include *I can't do this; I don't deserve success or happiness; I'll never make enough money to retire; I'm too old to start something new; I don't have time or the money to be healthy.* The irony is that so many people think they can't change, and yet change is inevitable.

Growth comes when we embrace change rather than resist it. Shift your perspective from fearing change to seeing it as an opportunity. Leaning into change opens doors to new possibilities.

Take action within the next twenty-four hours. You need to take a step to move forward today. In *Atomic Habits,* James Clear says, "You do not rise to the level of your goals. You fall to the level of your systems."[5]

Instead of focusing solely on big goals, create systems that support progress. For example, if your goal is to write a book, commit to writing for just ten minutes a day. If you want to exercise more, start with a five-minute walk.

One of the best ways to ensure follow-through is to make your goal public. Studies show that people are more likely to achieve their goals when they share them with others and ask for accountability. Tell someone your goal today and ask them to check in with you.

Become consistent. Momentum isn't built through occasional bursts of effort; it's created through consistent action. This is why setting small, achievable goals is crucial. When we focus on big, overwhelming goals, we can end up paralyzed by inaction.

I love the analogy Darren Hardy uses in his seminar on overcoming overload. Imagine a massive staircase leading to your biggest goals. If you look up and stare at the top every day, it feels impossible to reach. But if you focus on just the next step and then the next, before you know it, you're halfway up the staircase.

Try some of the following suggestions to stay consistent: Use a habit tracker to measure progress; set reminders or schedule small, actionable steps; celebrate small wins to reinforce your progress; and remind yourself that consistency matters more than perfection.

Create a routine. Routine is often considered the cornerstone of self-discipline because it removes so much of the mental noise that slows people down. When you build a structured routine, you aren't waking up every day wondering what to do next or negotiating with yourself about whether you feel like it. You've already made the decisions ahead of time.

It's not about willpower. It's about habit. The more consistently you follow the routine, the easier it becomes to stick with it, even on the tough days.

If you're not sure where to start, choose one piece of your day—maybe the first fifteen minutes after you wake up or the thirty minutes before bed. Decide what you want that time to look like. Write it down and follow it for a week. The goal isn't perfection. It's showing up for yourself regularly enough that this small piece of your day starts to feel automatic.

Once that happens, it's much easier to build on it. Routines create structure, and structure creates freedom— the freedom to focus fully on your goals instead of wasting energy and deciding what to do next.

Find your flow. Momentum is closely tied to the concept of flow, which Mihaly Csikszentmihalyi describes in his book *Flow: The Psychology of Optimal Experience.*

Flow is a state of complete immersion and focus on an activity.[6]

When you're in flow, you experience heightened productivity and creativity because you are fully engaged. You're free from distractions and self-doubt. People in a state of flow lose track of time, feel deeply engaged in what they're doing, experience reduced fear and anxiety, and are more productive and creative.

One of the best ways to get into flow is to start with one focused task. Shut off all distractions, immerse yourself fully, and let your natural momentum carry you forward.

GET READY TO BREAK THROUGH INERTIA

Have you ever tried to push a heavy object that wasn't moving? The first moment—the effort required to break its stillness—is always the hardest. But once it starts moving, it becomes easier to keep it in motion. This is inertia, the principle in physics that states an object at rest stays at rest, and an object in motion stays in motion unless acted upon by an external force. In other words, starting is always the biggest challenge, but once you're in motion, momentum makes the process easier.

The same principle applies to your personal momentum. When you feel stuck, it can be because you're battling inertia—the resistance to change or movement. Here's the good news: Just like in physics, once you take action, it becomes significantly easier to keep moving forward.

In the next chapter, we'll explore how the science of momentum applies to your personal growth and success, breaking it down into five essential components: the need for an initial push, the power of consistency, the impact of friction, the importance of direction, and the surprising strength of small steps.

Once you begin to take action and start seeing the results, it's intoxicating. What was once difficult seems easier. What was once mundane actually might be fun. The consistent action over time creates confidence. And as confidence grows, you desire to take more action, and so the process goes.

You don't have to stay stuck. Momentum is waiting. It just needs a push.

THE PHYSICS OF MOMENTUM

Momentum is simple physics. But living it is anything but simple. An object at rest stays at rest. You've heard it. You may have also lived it from time to time.

For me, it showed up in my health. I wasn't in a weight range that put my life at risk, nor was I sitting on the couch eating donuts all day. But I was definitely what I'd call a dabbler in the realm of physical fitness and nutrition. I read books about longevity. I watched some incredible transformation stories that left me feeling inspired. But the excitement came in short bursts. Then I'd stall out again. The effort it took just to get moving—that first push—always felt heavier than I expected.

That's inertia.

It's not personal.

It's not about willpower, motivation, or discipline.

It's physics.

Objects at rest stay at rest until acted on by an outside force. Sometimes that force is a new plan, program, coach, or even a prescription if that's what gets the ball rolling. But once you break free from inertia and start stacking those small wins, everything starts to shift.

Momentum builds, and with it, the weight you felt at the beginning gets lighter.

I've had to remind myself (and maybe you need to hear this too) that we are capable of so much more than we know. This means you, no matter where you are right now. But capability doesn't mean much without action. That first action is always the hardest. Trust me. I've been there. Maybe you have too. Maybe that's why you're here right now.

You consider your next goal, and it feels massive, like standing at the base of a huge mountain. You tell yourself, "If this were really a priority, I'd be doing it already."

Sound familiar?

Let me say this: There's nothing wrong with having big goals. I encourage it. But if you're feeling overwhelmed, it's because you're focusing on the whole mountain instead of the first step. That's why I've learned to chunk it down into small goals and daily wins, one bite at a time.

James Clear talks about this in *Atomic Habits*. By lowering the barrier to entry—starting small—you remove the friction and make the first step easier. That's physics too.

Less friction equals easier momentum. And over time, those tiny actions compound into real momentum—the kind that reprograms your brain and shifts your self-image, not just your habits.[7]

I've seen it in my health, but also in my mortgage career. Early on, I hated cold calling. Most people do. In sales, we refer to it as call reluctance, the quiet, sneaky resistance salespeople feel toward making outreach, especially phone calls, even when we know it's the exact activity that creates results. It's not laziness, and it's not a lack of skill. It's psychological friction. The brain senses potential rejection, interruption, or embarrassment and throws up a speed bump disguised as "I should prep more," "I'll do this later," or "Let me check my email first." The behavior looks like avoidance, and the root is fear dressed up as productivity. But do you know the only cure for call reluctance?

That's right: calling.

The action itself—not the part where you think about it—is what breaks the hold of inertia. Every call makes the next one easier. Eventually, momentum takes over, and it feels natural.

Same physics. Different arena.

Here's what I want you to know: You don't have to feel ready to start. In fact, most of the time you won't. But action creates clarity. Action creates confidence. And action even messy, imperfect action—is the only thing that breaks the grip of inertia.

So let me ask you: What's your first push going to be?

WHEN MOMENTUM BECOMES AN ILLUSION

Being a lifelong learner is a good thing.

But if you never apply what you learn, you aren't going anywhere.

I've spent years fascinated by personal development—books, seminars, podcasts—you name it. I highlighted sections, took notes, and built plans. But more often than not, I got stuck in preparation mode. It felt like I was making progress, but nothing was actually happening. This is a sneaky trap called the illusion of momentum.

Here's how it plays out. First, you get fired up about a goal. Let's say you want to write a book. You start reading everything you can about strengthening your craft. You research productivity hacks, plot structures, and best-selling author habits. You even go as far as to see which notebooks and pens people use. You dive into podcasts, sign up for a few webinars, and maybe even take a masterclass or two or three.

That's inertia. It's not personal. It's not about willpower, motivation, or discipline. It's physics.

It feels like progress.

Your brain gets a little dopamine hit every time you learn something new. It tricks you into believing you're doing the work.

But then someone asks, "How's your book coming along? Can I see what you've written so far?"

And then you realize you haven't even written a single word.

All that motion, all that learning energy never actually left your head. You've been spinning in place, mistaking preparation for progress. And the longer you stay in that cycle, the harder it is to break out. That's physics too. You need to be the external force for yourself by taking action.

Don't get me wrong. This isn't a lecture or a way for me to stand on a pedestal and berate you. I've lived this more times than I can count, and I'd like to help you learn this lesson through my experiences.

In sales, in personal goals, and even in the way I approached coaching early on, I veered away from what I really wanted. I attended the conferences, paid for the coaching programs, and filled the notebooks with ideas and strategies. And hear me when I say this: It felt like momentum. It felt like I was doing the work.

But when I stepped back and asked myself, "What have I actually done with all this knowledge?" the answer was always the same: not much.

This is where things can get us off track. We often confuse potential energy with kinetic energy. Potential energy is all the learning, ideas, and good intentions. We gather it and store it. It's ready to go. But it doesn't help us until we convert it into kinetic energy, which is actual forward motion.

The more we learn without action, the more we train ourselves to feel productive without producing anything. This mental trap feels comfortable. After all, learning is safe and controlled. Action, on the other hand, can expose us. It comes with risks like mistakes, rejection, and failure. That internal friction can keep us in the learning loop.

I've caught myself thinking I'm better than I really am, not because of arrogance but because of this false sense of

You don't have to feel ready to start.

progress. I'd pat myself on the back for attending a conference, but the deals didn't close themselves. I'd read the books about fitness, but my body didn't change until I showed up for the workouts consistently.

Learning and doing need to go hand-in-hand. This is when you grow, learning more about yourself and where you want to go, and making progress toward your biggest goals.

But momentum isn't built by consuming only. It's built by creating.

This is another law of physics in action. Momentum—true momentum—is mass in motion. In other words, you have to be moving for momentum to exist. And the more consistently you move, the more momentum builds. But without action, you're just storing up potential energy that never gets released.

Here's my challenge to you: What is the thing you keep researching, preparing for, or getting ready to do?

What's one action you've been putting off because learning feels safer?

Don't misunderstand me. Learning is valuable, no doubt. But learning without doing is just a form of intellectual entertainment. In today's world of information and AI, it is very common to gain knowledge without applying it.

If you want real momentum, you have to step out of the safe space of learning and into the real work of doing. That's where confidence lives. That's where momentum takes hold. The first step is the hardest. But it's also the only way forward.

WHEN LIFE HAPPENS

I'm not some kind of rock star who is killing it at work and in life every single day. I'm just like everybody else. Some mornings, I wake up and don't feel like getting up right away. I don't want to make calls.

The thing about momentum of any kind is that it doesn't care how you feel. It doesn't care if you're tired or frustrated, or if life just gut-punched you for no good reason. It only responds to one thing—movement. It's not personal. It's not emotional. It's just cause and effect. You move and it builds. You stop, and it slows to a stop too. That's the rule.

If you've ever had to push a car that's stalled, you know exactly what I'm talking about. Getting it to

Learning without doing is just a form of intellectual entertainment.

budge even a couple of inches feels impossible at first. You lean your whole body into it, gritting your teeth, and for what feels like forever, it just sits there stuck. But then it shifts just the tiniest bit, and you realize something. Once the first little bit of momentum kicks in, it's still work, but the car starts cooperating. It rolls with you, not against you. But if you stop pushing too long, it settles right back into stuck, and you have to fight for that first inch forward all over again.

That's exactly how life works when you're building a business, chasing a goal, or trying to level up. Momentum doesn't care if you had a bad day or if you're tired of trying. It only tracks whether you're moving. And the reality is, you will have bad days. We all do. Those are the days when the work you do feels like it weighs a hundred pounds on your shoulders and you'd rather do anything else—days when you can't even convince yourself to sit at your desk, much less knock out your to-do list.

On those days, the easiest thing in the world is to tell yourself, *I deserve a break.* And hey, sometimes you do. Life happens, and you've got to give yourself some grace. But there's a thin line between a well-earned break and a self-inflicted rut. You have to be honest with yourself about which side you're on.

I've had to get really good at asking myself hard questions, especially when I feel stuck. *How much time did I actually work today? How much of it was real work, and how much was scrolling social media or getting sucked into a Netflix rabbit hole? Did I get enough sleep, or did*

I stay up too late doing things that won't get me closer to where I want to be?

Most of us give ourselves way too much credit for being busy, but if we're honest, we're not doing nearly as much as we think. If you're willing to have that honest conversation—without beating yourself up over your observations—that's where you take your power back.

Even on those tough days, you still have to find a way to get your head right and get back in the game. I've created a whole arsenal of tricks I can lean on when I'm dragging. It starts with my mindset. I'll run through my affirmations—little reminders I've built up over the years that help me shift out of whatever funk I'm in and back into the headspace of someone

> **Momentum doesn't care if you had a bad day or if you're tired of trying. It only tracks whether you're moving.**

who gets things done. It is important to note, though, that affirmations don't replace action. They remind us of who we are while we take action.

If the words aren't cutting it for me? That's when the music comes in.

There's nothing like some good old-fashioned heavy metal to shake me out of a slump. I log into my SiriusXM and choose Hair Nation Top 100. I've got some go-to tracks like Autograph's "Turn Up the Radio" or AC/DC's "Back in Black." Those kinds of songs hit you right in the chest and say, *Get up and move.* I'll crank it loud (in my earbuds so my coworkers don't hear it), sometimes walking around my office or jumping up and down just to snap myself out of my own head.

Another one I like to listen to and dance to in the morning is "Do the Hustle" by Van McCoy. It's from the year I was born: 1975. It's nearly impossible to play that song without moving your body to the beat.

If that's not enough, I'll pull up a few of my favorite YouTube videos of big-name speakers who know how to light a fire under you and remind you why you started in the first place. One of my favorite apps at the time of this writing is PEP. All I have to do is open it up, and it gives me a much-needed pep talk.

But the key isn't just getting hyped up. It's about accountability. I don't just rely on a feeling to get me moving again. I've got systems in place to help. I have one spreadsheet designated to track everything I need to do before noon. When I'm off-track, I can't hide

Because momentum's waiting, and it's only going to show up when I do.

from it. It's right there, staring me in the face. That's what keeps me honest—a combination of loud '80s and '90s hair bands, affirmations, a good dose of inspiration from YouTube, and a system that doesn't let me lie to myself about how much I'm accomplishing.

That's why I love sports so much—especially golf and baseball. Every round of golf is made up of individual holes, and every hole adds up to your final score. You're going to have bad holes—guaranteed. You're going to hook one into the water and completely shank a shot. But it's just one hole. You still have the next one. It's the same thing in baseball—you can strike out in the first inning, but you'll be back up to bat. There's always another swing.

That's life. There's always another swing if you take it. That's the difference. You can't afford to let one bad day turn into a bad week, then a bad month, and then a bad year. You have to treat it like a bad hole of golf. Shake it off, take a lap, get your head right, and step up to the next tee. You don't have to be perfect. But you do have to keep swinging.

I'll allow myself a cheat day now and then, but no cheat weeks or months. I might miss a step, but I give myself some grace and consider how I'm going to get moving again. I'll tap into my go-to strategies and make a choice. I'll put on a new song, get my mind right, and maybe even go for a walk if I need to, and then it's back to it because momentum's waiting, and it's only going to show up when I do.

CONSISTENCY IS KEY

If you want to build momentum in your life, you can't just rely on luck, talent, or motivation. None of those things will carry you far enough.

So what does?

Consistency.

Showing up over and over again, even when you don't feel like it, when you're tired, or when you aren't seeing progress—that's the real secret.

In science, momentum is mass multiplied by velocity—how much something weighs multiplied by how fast it's moving. The more consistently that object moves, the more energy it collects and the harder it becomes to stop. Think about a train leaving the station. It starts off slowly, barely creeping along. But give it enough time and consistent power, and that thing is going to need miles of space to bring it to a halt.

Our lives work the same way—our goals, our personal growth, our careers—all of it. When you take small, consistent steps forward, you build momentum. The hardest part is getting started. Yes, I've said that before, but hear me out. The second hardest part is staying in motion when it feels like nothing is happening. This is where a lot of us get tripped up. But here's the truth: Something *is* happening.

Every small action feeds the momentum machine, even when you can't see it yet.

If you want proof, watch the movie *The Pursuit of Happyness*. It's such an incredible film because it's so real and raw. It isn't just some feel-good story. It's about what it actually takes to change the trajectory of your life. If you've never seen it, go watch it right now if you don't want the spoilers.

Will Smith plays Chris Gardner, a guy who goes from selling medical devices and sleeping in public restrooms to landing a spot in a prestigious brokerage firm. And he doesn't get that job because of luck or because he decided he wanted something and just waited for it to show up for him. He gets the job because he refuses to stop moving.[8]

Let me be clear. Chris had every excuse to quit. He was homeless. He was raising his young son on his own. He was broke. Any reasonable person would have understood if he gave up and looked for a different job somewhere else. But he didn't.

He kept showing up, making phone calls, and finding a way to dig deep and keep working. Sometimes he showed up with no sleep, no food, and not knowing if he and his son would make it into the homeless shelter line before it was full for the night. And when he went into the corporate office for a meeting about the one job they had to offer, he looked a mess.

He had just painted the apartment he got evicted from and didn't have time to change or clean up and still make it on time. When they offered him the job, he put his head in his hands and sobbed. His consistency made his relentless dream a reality. It finally paid off.

That's momentum in action.

Here's the part I really need you to understand: Most of the people who applied didn't get the job. Chris got the one spot, but dozens of other people walked out of that office building with nothing to show for all the work they'd put in.

And that's life.

Not everyone is going to get the gold star just because they want it. But those people weren't failures. They walked away with something just as valuable: experience, growth, and proof that they could show up and give their all.

And that matters.

Creating momentum in your life isn't just about winning the prize. It's about who you become in the process. Every phone call Chris made strengthened his persistence muscles. Every rejection made him a little more resilient. Every time he swallowed his pride and got in line for food or a safe place for his son and himself to sleep, he was reinforcing the habit of taking action no matter what. And that's the habit that changes everything.

This is where so many of us can go wrong. We think momentum comes from some magical burst of inspiration, that one moment where everything clicks into place and the path is clear. But it's not as exciting in reality. Momentum comes from taking action before you feel ready and continuing even after the spark of inspired action comes and goes.

The habits you created, the resilience you built, and the skills you sharpened all come with you.

This is why consistency matters more than perfect action. It's not about nailing every step. It's about taking the next one and still moving forward. It's the accumulation of those steps that creates your momentum.

Let's go back to physics for a second. The formula for momentum doesn't just apply to objects; it applies to you. In this case, your mass is everything you've built up so far—your skills, experiences, past failures and wins, your reputation, all of it. Your velocity is how consistently you're moving forward. The bigger your mass—the more experience and resilience you've built—the more impact you create when you apply consistent action.

But the reverse is also true. If you stop moving, your velocity drops to zero. Your momentum dies. It doesn't matter how much potential energy you have. If you're not consistently taking action, you have no momentum. And restarting from zero? That's way harder than just staying in motion.

This is why you can't afford to quit when things get hard. And trust me, things will get hard. There will be days when it feels pointless. Days when you don't see progress. Days when you're certain you're wasting your time. Those days are exactly where momentum is made or lost. If you push through, even with the tiniest action, you keep your momentum alive. If you stop, even for a little while, you lose way more than you realize.

Here's the part some of us miss. We're never just working toward one goal. Even if you didn't get the job, the promotion, or the big break you wanted, the momentum you built doesn't disappear. It rolls along with you to the next opportunity. The habits you created, the resilience you built, and the skills you sharpened all come with you. Every bit of effort compounds.

CREATE YOUR SYSTEMS

To avoid inertia, it's important to have systems in place before you need them. You can't rely on how you feel in the moment to decide whether or not you're going to move forward. As you know by now, momentum doesn't care how you feel, and it definitely doesn't wait for you to feel motivated. If you're serious about where you want to go, start creating the habits, triggers, and systems so you don't lose time getting stuck in your own head.

The following list isn't exhaustive but may inspire you to create your own list of systems that will work best. Take a moment to consider these options to keep you moving in the right direction, no matter what the circumstances.

Ponder your playlist. Music is one of the fastest ways to shift your state of mind. When you're flatlining emotionally and having one of those days when you can't even think about tackling the next task, music can bypass all the excuses and hit you right in the nervous system. For this reason, you need a go-to playlist—not one you built when you were already stuck but one you create in advance when you're clear-headed and focused.

> **Motion creates emotion, and emotion influences motion. That's the loop.**

You know some of the artists on mine. Those hair bands always make me feel like anything is possible. Maybe for you it's hip-hop, classical, country, jazz—it doesn't matter what it is as long as it makes you feel like getting up and doing something.

This isn't just about entertainment. It's a strategy. Your playlist is a tool. It's a switch you can flip when you need to pull yourself out of a slump. We all have those mornings when we'd rather stay in bed. When it feels like things aren't going the way I imagined, I can crank up the volume and force some life back into my body.

Motion creates emotion, and emotion influences motion. That's the loop. On those days, you can't sit around and wait for a spark. You have to start the fire yourself.

Set up your spreadsheet. I'm a big believer that if you want something to get done, you have to see it—not in some abstract, vision board kind of way. I mean real, tangible tasks, tracked in black and white, where I can't lie to myself. I've learned that if it's not tracked, it most likely won't get done.

That's why I created a Before Noon Spreadsheet. Every day, I have a list of non-negotiables—things I need to do before noon, no matter what else is happening. I understand that I am most productive in the mornings. In the afternoon, my motivation and productivity tend to go down. It's my personal scoreboard, and it keeps me honest.

When you feel inertia creeping in, it's easy to convince yourself you're busy when you're just spinning your wheels. This spreadsheet doesn't care about excuses. It's either done or it's not. And when you see those empty boxes without checkmarks in them at 11:45 a.m., you either scramble to check them off or you sit with the reality that you're the only reason you're not moving forward.

Your spreadsheet doesn't have to look like mine. It needs to be yours—tailored to your goals, your priorities, and your reality. Build it before you need it so on the days when you don't feel like you can trust your brain, you can still trust your system.

Fill the wall. One of the most powerful systems I ever created came from a simple phrase: *Fill the wall.* It started years ago when I felt stuck and doubted if I was cut out for the life I wanted. I realized I needed constant visual reminders of what I was working toward—not just once in a while, but all the time.

I started writing quotes, goals, lessons—anything that lit a fire under me—and taped them to my wall. Over time, the wall filled up, and something changed. Whenever I felt that creeping inertia, all I had to do was glance at the wall. It was like my past self was there, reminding me why I couldn't quit.

This isn't just decoration. It's a system. You're building your own personal Hall of Fame. It's a wall that reflects who you're becoming and why it matters. It's the ultimate anti-inertia insurance policy.

Don't think about failure. This isn't about perfection. It's about refusing to let inertia win by default. Bad days happen. We'll screw up, miss targets, and have deals fall apart. Welcome to being human! But we cannot allow ourselves to stack failure on top of failure.

One bad day? Fine. One bad week? Absolutely not.

If you miss your goals today, your system has to include a plan to reset tomorrow. Whether it's a morning run, a brain dump journal, or a standing call with a friend who will call you out, you need a mechanism to pull you back onto the field after you've been knocked down.

The key is not giving yourself too much grace. Yes, be kind to yourself. But understand that kindness doesn't mean coddling. There's a big difference between understanding why you fell down and deciding to stay there. Forgive the bad day. Forbid the bad week.

Break the pattern of rumination. If we let our brains do whatever they want when we're struggling, they're going to take us down a rabbit hole of excuses, doubts, and stories about why we can't. That's inertia's best trick: convincing us that thinking about the problem counts as solving it.

You need a hard stop when you catch yourself ruminating. I have a personal rule: When I catch myself replaying the same worry for the third time, I have to do something productive. Anything. It can be sending an email, making a call, or writing down three options for how to move forward—whatever gets me out of my head and into action.

Rumination is inertia dressed up like problem-solving. Don't fall for it. The only way forward is through action, and your system should always default to *doing* rather than over*thinking*.

The systems you've built are powerful, but they're only part of the equation. Even with the best tools, momentum can still stall when internal roadblocks show up.

Doubts, excuses, and unresolved baggage can creep in when things get tough.

Next, we'll identify momentum disruptors. The goal is not just to power through but to recognize what's really holding you back so you can clear the path and keep moving forward.

CHAPTER 4

OVERCOMING YOUR MOMENTUM DISRUPTORS

How many times have you picked up a self-help book from some new thought leader and thought, *Man, this person is such a go-getter. They're always on their A-game. Always successful. Always making money.*

This isn't one of those books.

I admire those people, but that isn't real life from where I'm sitting. Real life means living out our biggest dreams despite the messiness. It's recognizing that life involves managing and coping with the disruptors we can't always control while still finding a way to keep moving forward and building momentum toward what we want.

Don't get me wrong. I'm not trying to create a book that is a major downer. But I'm not interested in pretending to be something I'm not. Life happens. We all have stuff we go through. Some of us are better at putting on a brave face and pretending like everything is fine. And sometimes we're exhausted as the sun goes down because we spent all day trying to ignore our feelings.

As I write this chapter, my family is facing some challenges in this season of our lives. As a father, there's only so much I can do for my kids. As a husband, I can only offer so much to my wife. And right now, I'm questioning whether I'm making the right choices for any of us. I'm supposed to be the provider, the steady one. It's hard to sit with the feeling that I might be falling short, unable to support the people I love in the way they each need. At work, my thoughts drift to home. At home, I can't stop thinking about work.

It would be very easy to give in to all the obstacles tugging at my attention and walk away from my relentless dream of becoming an author. But I truly believe that this is the book I need to both share and hear during this time in my life.

Maybe you're juggling something right now and feel like a circus performer racing back and forth to keep plates spinning on their sticks. Just as you steady one, another one wobbles dangerously at the other end. It's exhausting, but you know if you stop for even a moment, everything could come crashing down.

Before you can reclaim your focus and build momentum, you have to confront the disruptors that are holding you back. Ignoring the forces weighing you down is like trying to climb a mountain with stones in your backpack. The weight doesn't just slow you down; it can change the trajectory of your path altogether. It can force you to compensate, overcompensate, or even freeze. What makes this journey even harder is that these disruptors are not always external. Some of the most challenging disruptors are within you.

The good news is that we always have hope. And if we can keep an open mind and look for the signs of the most common momentum disruptors, we always have the power to choose something different. We'll start by going deeper into momentum disruptors. I'll also share my favorite strategies to regain your focus and get your momentum moving again.

> **Rumination is inertia dressed up like problem-solving.**

NEGATIVE THOUGHT PATTERNS

As humans, we're great at taking a single moment and spinning it into a worst-case scenario. That's called catastrophizing. Something unexpected happens, and within seconds, we've imagined total collapse. It's easy to go from calm to full-blown crisis mode. We create elaborate stories about our struggles, and most of them never happen. But we live like they will. That stress lodges itself in our bodies. It keeps us up at night. It shows up in tension headaches, shallow breathing, tight shoulders, and even nausea. And still, we keep spinning those stories, convincing ourselves they're real.

Jennifer Taitz makes a powerful distinction between stress and anxiety in her book *Stress Resets*. She says stress is a disruption to our emotional or physiological balance. It's the "life happens" moment. Anxiety is more like worry on repeat, often disconnected from reality but very much fueled by our thoughts. And here's the part that hit me. She writes, "When life feels overwhelming, human beings often instinctively do things that end up making us, or the situation, feel worse."[9] Think procrastinating, snapping at people we care about, numbing out with our phones, food, or substances. These knee-jerk reactions don't solve the problem; they keep us stuck.

The truth is that stress is part of a meaningful life. Roy Baumeister, a psychologist Taitz references, said it well: "Meaningful involvements increase one's stress."[10]

Until we learn to observe our thoughts and choose to take control of them, we'll keep creating the outcomes we fear most.

But that's not a reason to avoid meaning. It's a reason to build resilience. He goes on to say, "Think about it: To design a life with zero stress, you'd have to shrink the scope of what you do, willfully denying life's realities and avoiding anything remotely challenging."[11]

Finding ways to build resilience is where Taitz's "stress resets" come in. They are small, actionable ways to shift your state without waiting for life to settle down.

And most importantly, they help us restore what we lose when we're overwhelmed: a sense of hope. Taitz writes:

> The more you practice regulating intense feelings, the more you'll experience a growing sense of possibility and be able to tap into something we all need these days: hope. Hope isn't just a transient feeling. It hinges on having a clear life purpose and a willingness to persist in moving forward toward that purpose.[12]

That's what we're after—not perfection but forward motion. And hope is what makes it sustainable.

We have to be mindful of our thoughts. I'll be the first to tell you that's far easier said than done. But the truth is, we actually do have control over what we think. I could write an entire book on the importance of thoughts alone.

The thing about the mind is that it's incredibly creative. The more you dwell on certain thoughts and allow them to ruminate, the more freedom you give them to grow and morph into those worst-case scenarios. Here's the truth: Most of those thoughts aren't probable or based in reality. But when you let your mind run wild, those made-up outcomes start to feel real. They create stress, anxiety, and probably some depression. All of this can chip away at your momentum until you feel like you're losing control.

The problem isn't just that our minds generate negative thoughts; it's that we get stuck in them. And we keep feeding the loop, often without realizing it. I was reminded of this recently when I read something from Cathryn Lavery at Best Self. She talked about how she'll watch a space documentary to reset her perspective when she feels stress building up. It may sound simple, but there is something powerful about it. Seeing that tiny pale blue dot floating in the vastness of space can snap you out of your mental spiral. It can remind you of how small your day-to-day problems really are. That shift can help break the grip of anxiety.

It also made me think of something Robert Greene wrote about how we poison our own minds, not through any dramatic event but by constantly reacting to external noise. We scroll, consume, and engage with drama that has nothing to do with us. And we call it being informed, but it's really an emotional contagion. We're not collecting useful information. We're catching other people's stress.[13]

In times of uncertainty, focusing on what you can control isn't just helpful; it's essential. That's why we need to get honest with ourselves about what's happening in our own minds. We have to recognize when we're catastrophizing or building an entire life story around something that hasn't even happened. We have to be willing to call ourselves out, and it isn't always easy.

Until we learn to observe our thoughts and choose to take control of them, we'll keep creating the outcomes we fear most. At the very least, we'll derail ourselves and lose the momentum we worked so hard to gain. We can't control our thoughts by brute force. It's about awareness, recognition, and redirection. In those moments of despair, we have to acknowledge our thoughts as not self-serving.

We have to call them out for what they are: noise, static, and mental interference.

This isn't a one-and-done fix. It's a process of acknowledging the negativity and choosing to redirect your thoughts toward something more productive. And it is possible. When you can regain control over your mind, you also create the space to get moving again.

DISRUPTORS THAT DERAIL US

Before we can move forward with clarity and momentum, we have to confront what's holding us back. Disruptors—both internal and external—can quietly derail even our best efforts. Some are obvious, like a crisis or a toxic relationship. Others are more hidden, like limiting beliefs or unresolved emotional pain. In this section, we'll look at four major disruptors: unprocessed pain, internal barriers, external disruptors, and disconnection from your true self. Once you can name them, you can start to move through them.

UNPROCESSED PAIN

Unprocessed pain is a powerful disruptor. Emotional wounds that haven't been acknowledged, healed, or integrated don't just fade away with time. They become embedded in your thoughts, habits, and reactions, rearing their heads at the worst possible moments. Like the day when you're at the store, and you suddenly feel enraged at the person who gets in the "ten items or less" line with fifteen items. It feels like that person's inability to count is the issue, but it's actually a trigger of something much deeper that you haven't worked through.

Childhood trauma, unfinished grief, unresolved anger, abandonment wounds, rejection, guilt, and shame can all fall into this category. You can try to push forward, but if that pain is still festering beneath the surface, it's like building a house on unstable ground. Grief that was never truly processed may resurface during stressful situations. Anger from betrayal can poison new relationships. Guilt and shame over past mistakes can fuel self-sabotage and paralyze progress.

In *The Body Keeps the Score,* Bessel van der Kolk explains how trauma lives in the body, creating patterns of tension, fear, and even physical illness when left unresolved. Emotional pain doesn't just evaporate. It mutates and grows until you deal with it.[14]

INTERNAL DISRUPTORS

Internal disruptors are the mental barriers that hold you back, even when everything around you seems like it's ready to progress. These are limiting beliefs, fears, and unresolved identity issues that often stem from old wounds or societal conditioning.

Erwin McManus suggests the most negative energy we can have is fear. What you fear establishes the boundaries of your personal freedom. For example, if you are afraid of people, you find yourself alone. If you are afraid of failure, you will stay right where you are. The freedom we desire is on the other side of your fears.[15]

Fear of failure can paralyze you before you even begin. But the fear of the outcomes from success can be just as disruptive. What if achieving your goals alienates you from the people you care about? What if stepping into your full potential means exposing yourself to scrutiny or criticism? Or what if you succeed and it's still not enough for you?

And it's not just fear. Anger that hasn't been processed can morph into resentment and blind you from seeing new opportunities. Holding onto bitterness or refusing to forgive someone who hurt you might feel like a way to protect yourself, but it keeps you emotionally handcuffed to past experiences. Anxiety keeps your nervous system in overdrive, convincing you that danger is always around the corner, even when it's not. Impatience makes you bail on the process before the progress has a chance to show up.

Then there's the victim mentality. It tells you the world is against you and that nothing is in your control. It robs you of your ability to take responsibility for your life. Cynicism and skepticism become shields that keep you from fully engaging with life if they're left unchecked. You may tell yourself you're being realistic, but deep down, it's a way to protect yourself from disappointment. And let's not forget the silent momentum killer: self-doubt. A lack of self-esteem can make you feel like you're never enough, even when all the evidence says otherwise.

These mental knots are incredibly difficult to untangle because they are rooted in your own perception of yourself and the world. In *Atomic Habits,* James Clear discusses how small mental shifts can lead to transformative change, but only if you're willing to confront the fears that hold you back. You can't always choose what happens to you, but you can choose how you respond. That choice starts by identifying the internal patterns you're putting in the driver's seat of your life.[16]

EXTERNAL DISRUPTORS

External disruptors are often easier to recognize but just as difficult to overcome as internal disruptors. These are the events and circumstances beyond your control. They could be financial setbacks, health issues, family struggles, toxic relationships, or an unstable work environment.

Even with the best mindset and preparation, life can throw unexpected challenges your way. The key is recognizing when these external factors are affecting your momentum rather than internalizing them as failures.

DISCONNECTION FROM YOUR TRUE SELF

This disruptor feels more like a compromise rather than a crisis. Disconnection from your true self happens when the life you're living doesn't match who you really are. It shows up in the feeling of being stuck in roles or routines that no longer serve you. Suppressed dreams, unhealthy relationship patterns, and a lack of clarity about your own desires fill this category.

You may find yourself living out someone else's expectations for your life while your own needs and passions remain unfulfilled and forgotten. Or you might be so caught up in your day-to-day grind that you lose sight of what truly matters to you.

Each of these disruptors has its own way of derailing your momentum. They don't vanish because you want them to. But identifying them is the first step to breaking free. You have to be willing to acknowledge the pain, challenge your own limiting beliefs, address external obstacles head-on, and realign your life with your true self. Because until you do, the path forward will always be littered with the remnants of what you haven't faced.

Understanding your disruptors is only part of the equation. What you do with that understanding is what matters most. It's time to regain your momentum. It's not about erasing your struggles altogether but learning how to see through them and learning what you can do to begin to loosen their grip on your momentum. Once you do, you open the door to focus, clarity, and momentum. And that's where your real journey begins.

CLEARING THE MECHANISM

Growing up in Texas, I played many sports, but the one that I loved the most and played the longest was baseball. So needless to say, many of my favorite movies revolve around baseball and the lessons that can be learned from sports. Here's an incredible movie that lends itself to figuring out a way to quiet all the noise and focus on just one thing.

Kevin Costner's character, Billy Chapel, in the movie *For Love of the Game,* is a professional pitcher near the end of his career. The movie shares his history of playing professional baseball and navigating a relationship as he works to stay present on the pitcher's mound during what we later find out is his final game.

Before the game begins, the club's owner lets Chapel know he's about to sell the team and suggests it might be time to retire so he doesn't get traded by the new ownership. We learn that Chapel's long-time girlfriend told him shortly before his meeting with the owner that she was moving out of the country. So right before he has to pitch, he has a lot of heavy thoughts going through his mind.

He steps onto the mound amidst all the chaos. The crowd is roaring. Fans are berating him. One voice makes its way to his ears: "You suck!" The weight of everything is pressing down on him. He drags his foot over the dirt and says, "Clear the mechanism." Once he speaks those words, the air around him warps, and everything but the batter and the catcher disappears. The noise fades. All the distractions in the stands vanish. It's just him, the ball, and the game.

That moment hits me because we've all been there, standing in our own versions of a high-stakes game, drowning in distractions, fighting to focus. The mental chatter can be deafening, full of fears, insecurities, outside opinions, and past failures. When momentum is disrupted, it's rarely because of external circumstances alone. It's the internal resistance, endless overthinking, and the stories we tell ourselves about why we can't do certain things that keep us stuck.[17]

When the mental static builds up, it's easy to spiral into inaction, to feel paralyzed by uncertainty. But here's the truth: Clarity isn't something you wait for. It's something you create. You *clear the mechanism* by taking control of your focus, shutting out the noise, and zeroing in on what actually moves you forward.

Most people assume that focus is about effort—trying harder, grinding longer, forcing yourself to push through distractions. But real focus, the kind that cuts through the noise and gets you moving again, isn't about effort. It's about elimination. It's about recognizing what doesn't belong in your headspace and intentionally shutting it out. It's about deciding what deserves your attention and refusing to let anything else take up space.

Clarity isn't something you wait for. It's something you create.

When you get stuck, ask yourself, *What's the loudest voice in my head right now?* Is it self-doubt? A past mistake? Someone else's expectations? Pain that never seems to end? Then ask, *Does this voice help me move forward, or is it keeping me stuck?* If it's the latter, it's time to clear it out.

Hear me when I say that I know some pain doesn't just vanish when you tell it to, even in the movies. There is a point when Billy Chapel's shoulder hurts so much that when he tries to clear the mechanism, the crowd and the noise start to fade, but less than a second later, it all comes back. When the pain you're experiencing hits a certain threshold, it can warp your ability to clear the mechanism. It's hard to focus when your body is screaming at you that something is wrong. In those moments, it takes everything you've got just to get through the day, let alone chase down a goal.

This isn't about ignoring reality or pretending challenges don't exist. It's about keeping them out of the driver's seat. It's about training your mind to focus on what is in your control instead of spiraling over everything that isn't. When Billy Chapel clears the mechanism, he doesn't erase his problems. He just refuses to let them dictate his next move. That's what regaining focus looks like in real life. You acknowledge the disruptors, and then you deliberately decide they do not get to control your momentum.

Clearing the mechanism isn't something you do once and master for the rest of your life. It's a habit, a skill, a decision you make repeatedly. It's about choosing to tune out what doesn't serve you and zeroing in on what does. It's getting out of your own head long enough to take the next step. Remember, this journey you're on isn't about perfection. It's about movement. And movement only happens when you quiet the noise and focus on the next pitch you're going to throw.

GET YOUR FOCUS BACK

So what can you do? You can't always clear the mechanism on your own, and that's alright. It's okay to get help when you need it. Here are some of the tools I've been successful with in those moments when I needed to get my focus back. Like the other lists before it, it isn't exhaustive, but it's a start. They aren't magical overnight solutions but rather practical steps backed by science and experience. Try them out and see what works best for you.

Practice breathwork. Let's talk about something you're probably doing right now without realizing it: holding your breath. Take a second to check in with yourself. Are you breathing deeply as you read this, or are you kind of holding it, using just enough oxygen to get by?

There's a name for this. It's called email apnea. It's an unconscious habit of shallow breathing or flat-out breath-holding while you're locked in on your phone, laptop, or to-do list. Research says around 80 percent of us do this regularly, especially when we're focused or stressed. That little habit might not seem like a big deal, but it messes with your oxygen levels and trips your stress response like a silent alarm going off in your body all day long.[18]

What's wild is that this isn't just a physical thing. It's deeply tied to your psychology. How long you can hold your breath actually connects to how well you handle discomfort. It's been studied as a measure of distress tolerance. So the way you breathe (or don't) can be a mirror for how you deal with stress, pressure, or emotional overload.

When you hold your breath or breathe shallowly for too long, you're not just depriving your brain of oxygen. You're triggering your body to stay in fight-or-flight mode. That means your mind races faster and your focus fractures. And your momentum? It tanks.

Here's the good news: This is something you can change. With simple breathwork techniques, you can reset your nervous system, reclaim your calm, and recenter your focus. It's not just woo-woo wellness advice. It's science-backed and practical. If you want to stop reacting and start consciously responding to your distractors, start with your breath.

The fix isn't some thirty-minute breathing session or a brand-new morning routine. It's simpler and more doable in the middle of a messy day. If you catch yourself bracing or locked up, just run a few physiological sighs. Inhale through your nose and then add a second shorter inhale right at the top. Then let it all out slowly through your mouth. Fully. Let your shoulders drop as you soften your chest. Do it again, as many times as it takes.

This technique helps you tell your nervous system it's safe to come out of high-alert mode. You're lowering your cortisol and shifting gears. As neuroscientist Andrew Huberman says, "The physiological sigh is a fast and effective way to calm down."[19]

I do a lot of breathwork, usually Huberman's technique, typically at the top of every hour. I've created a practice over the years to make sure I'm getting enough oxygen. I don't need to set a timer every hour because at this point, I've done it so often that it has become a natural part of my days. I also use it when I notice myself feeling overwhelmed by the stressors I'm dealing with. Whatever the reason, breathwork has become an easy way for me to slow down and refocus.

The next time you feel stuck, tense, or out of sync, interrupt the pattern with your breath as the signal. Or start by setting a timer to remind yourself to breathe periodically and see how you feel once you've developed a new habit. When you do, you're not just calming your body, you're building momentum again.

Try healthy distractions. Sometimes your mind just needs a break. When you're caught in a loop of stress or overthinking, one of the best things you can do is intentionally shift your focus. James Clear talks about the power of small, achievable actions that can help you break a negative cycle before it gains momentum and takes you in the wrong direction.[20]

I'd like to share something Anna Lembke says in *Dopamine Nation* because it makes a lot of sense. She explains how the brain is constantly trying to balance pleasure and pain. When we're deep in a stress spiral, it's often because that balance is off. We're swimming in discomfort without anything to anchor us. But here's the twist: Lembke says the way back to balance isn't to numb out; it's to lean into healthy discomfort. Exercise, creating something, journaling, even taking a cold shower can help.

They aren't escapes; they're tools, and the discomfort they bring can actually help restore our mental clarity.[21]

Journaling has been a go-to healthy distraction for me. There's something powerful about taking what's swirling around in your head and putting it on paper. It gets all those thoughts and feelings out of your system and makes space for something better.

Here's the point: Not all distractions are bad. The right ones can get your mind unstuck and back on track. We all know we can't wait for motivation to magically show up. Move your body, pick up a pen, take a walk. Do something that nudges you forward.

Stay present. Eckart Tolle's book *The Power of Now* drives home something we all need to hear more often: Presence isn't optional. If your mind is always stuck in the past or reaching toward the future, you're going to miss the life that's happening right in front of you. The only real power you have is in this moment. Right now.[22]

When I need to clear the mechanism and come back to center, one of the first places I turn to is nature. The sound of wind moving through trees, the warmth of the sun on my skin—those tiny, easily overlooked details have a way of anchoring you. They force you to slow down and really notice what's happening. That simple act of mindfulness won't solve everything, but it can stop the runaway train of anxious thoughts before they derail your entire day.

Another tool I use might sound unconventional, but it works. I'll stand on a vibration platform, close my eyes, and just focus on my muscles as they respond to the vibration. Having my eyes closed challenges my balance, which means I can't think about anything else. I have to be present and hyperfocused. That focus quiets the noise in my head. I don't have room to worry about anything. I'm just there, in my body, holding steady. The bonus is that the vibration plate isn't just about mindfulness and presence. From what I've read, it can help strengthen muscles, support lymphatic drainage, and improve circulation and bone density. Some even say it helps lower cortisol and reduce anxiety. For me, the biggest win is the stillness it forces through movement.

If you're looking for a way to come back to the moment and reset your mental state without needing to run off into the woods, this might be it. Presence doesn't have to be poetic. Sometimes it's just you standing still, doing the hard work of showing up for your life.

Consider what you consume. In his book *Digital Minimalism,* Cal Newport talks about the importance of being intentional about what you allow into your mind. This doesn't just mean limiting your social media intake but also being selective about the books you read, the conversations you have, and the environments you expose yourself to. It's all too easy to feed the negative stories with unhealthy inputs. All of it adds up, and most of it happens passively. Instead, curate what you consume to support your mental well-being and growth.[23]

I was speaking at a sales meeting recently and overheard a group of colleagues talking about the latest shows they were watching. A few of them were hooked on the kind of high-stress medical dramas that are basically designed to spike your adrenaline. These shows aren't just intense; they're engineered to pull you into emotional chaos. What struck me is how many of us consume this kind of content right before bed without realizing the effect it's having on us.

Your brain can't fully distinguish between fantasy and reality. When you're watching something stressful, your brain still processes it as real. That kind of repeated stimulation can leave you feeling more anxious, more reactive, and more prone to catastrophizing. Even if you don't consciously remember the details, your brain stores them.

Here's the good news: It works in the opposite direction too. There are shows, songs, and stories that lift you up, calm your nervous system, and shift your mindset. A show like *Ted Lasso* is full of optimism, humility, and emotional intelligence. When you consume things that reinforce positive values, you walk away feeling better, not worse.

That's why your morning and nightly routines matter so much. The first and last things you consume each day leave a lasting imprint. So if you're starting or ending your day with emotionally charged news, conflict-ridden shows, or passive scrolling through negativity, it's affecting your momentum whether you realize it or not.

Curate what you consume. Choose inputs that match the energy and clarity you want in your life. Be the gatekeeper of your mental space because your brain is paying attention, whether you think it is or not.

Give yourself a reality check. Research shows that interventions that increase perceived control over stressors and shift attention toward controllable aspects of experience—such as thoughts and behaviors—are associated with reductions in anxiety and negative affect.[24]

Interventions designed to modify how people respond to their thoughts and redirect attention away from uncontrollable sources of stress (e.g., metacognitive training) have been shown to reduce clinical anxiety.[25]

Harvard stress researchers have noted that repeatedly checking the news—especially more than eight times a day—creates a cognitive overload that impairs decision-making during uncertain times. People who limited themselves to one or two updates a day reported clearer thinking and better emotional regulation. The more noise you consume, the less you trust your own ability to act.[26]

Anna Katharina Schaffner contributed an article to *Positive Psychology* that describes life as three concentric circles. The inner circle is everything you can control: your thoughts, breath, and habits. The middle circle is what you can influence: your relationships and your environment. And the outer circle is the stuff you can only be aware of: world events, social media drama, other people's opinions. Most of us spend way too much time out there in the noise. It kills our clarity. The goal is to redirect your energy inward toward the things you can shape so you can actually build the kind of life you want instead of just reacting to the one being thrown at you.[27]

Engage the 10-10-10 rule. This one is short and sweet. When you find yourself stressing about something, it can help you put the experience into perspective. Ask yourself, *Will this problem matter in ten days? Ten months? Ten years?* It may not help you solve the problem, but it can help you understand where it fits into the bigger picture.

The 10-10-10 rule comes from Suzy Welch, former editor-in-chief of the *Harvard Business Review*. In a speech she gave at the Nordic Business Forum in 2013, she spoke about receiving accolades from other people who implemented this strategy once she wrote about it in *O* magazine for an article about work-life balance. She began to wonder why it worked so well and why people were giving her such intense feedback, telling her the 10-10-10 rule saved their lives. This is what she realized:

> 10-10-10 works so well because it forces you (if you're using it right) to come to terms with what really matters to you. . . . If you can come to terms with, get transparent about, and admit to yourself what your values are . . . and then do 10-10-10, that's when it's transformative.[28]

To dial in on your values, Welch suggests asking yourself three questions. (1) Fast forward to your seventy-fifth (or ninety-fifth) birthday. What would make you cry with regret? (2) What do you want people to say about you when you're not in the room? (3) What did you love/not love about your childhood? When you can make decisions that match your values, you're more able to live what she calls a happy, authentic life "because there's no such thing as a happy, phony life."[29]

Most of the things that hijack your momentum in the moment are temporary turbulence rather than long-term storms. When you realize that, it's easier to stay calm, refocus, and keep moving forward with intention instead of spiraling into panic. Perspective won't eliminate the stress, but it can definitely keep it out of the driver's seat.

Seek help. Some of the disruptors we've talked about are things you can start to shift with mindset work, breathwork, or changes in your habits. They're challenging but manageable when you commit to the process. But here's the truth: Not everything can be handled solo. And that's okay.

There are times when clearing the mechanism requires more than grit. It requires help. Therapy, medical support, or even opening up to someone you trust can be the difference between staying stuck and finally moving forward. Sometimes you need an outside perspective to cut through the painful fog and remind you what's real.

It isn't a sign of weakness or failure. It's a way to create a strategic plan to protect your momentum. Left unaddressed, pain can cloud your thinking, distort your perception, and make the path forward almost impossible to see. But when you take steps to manage the pain, whether it's physical, emotional, or spiritual, you give yourself room to breathe. You make space for clarity and start to shift from surviving to thriving.

A recent Forbes Health survey of 2,000 US adults found that nearly half of every generation now sees mental health as something worth prioritizing. And 67 percent of younger adults (18–27) and 66 percent of Baby Boomers (59–77) say we should be talking more openly about mental health with our friends.[30] That's a big shift from just a few decades ago. It means the idea of getting help isn't just getting accepted; it's moving closer toward getting normalized.

The most encouraging part of the survey is that the majority of younger adults said they strongly believe in the value of therapy. Even among the older crowd, people agree that it's important. Here's the bottom line: No matter your age or background, there's no shame in talking to a professional. In fact, it might be one of the smartest things you can do to get clear, get focused, and get going again. You're not alone, and you do not have to figure it all out by yourself.

If you're feeling like you've tried everything and you're still spinning your wheels, maybe it's time to seek help. The strongest thing you can do is say, "I can't do this alone." Because the moment you get the right kind of help is often the moment everything starts to change for the better.

MORE THAN AWARENESS

Your momentum disruptors are real, and they won't disappear overnight. But just recognizing them is a huge step forward. It's finally turning the lights on in a dark room. You can see what's holding you back. Now it's about clearing the path.

So where do you go from here? You've identified the disruptors that keep you spinning your wheels. And now it's time to break free from the hold they have over you. It isn't enough to know what's holding you back. Awareness on its own can't help you get your momentum moving forward again. You have to decide to do something about it. It's about getting your hands dirty, digging into your patterns, and confronting them head-on. It's about letting go of the stories that don't serve you and rewriting them so they do.

It's about letting go of the stories that don't serve you and rewriting them so they do.

You can't outrun the things that weigh you down. Even if you manage to sprint away from them for a while, they'll eventually catch up. The next step is all about action. It's about breaking free from the habits and mechanisms that keep you stuck. Momentum isn't created by accident. It's built with intention, grit, and a willingness to confront the things that make you uncomfortable.

In the next chapter, we'll dive into something that can hit close to home: the ways self-sabotage and self-medication can come into play when people are just trying to get by. Sometimes the biggest disruptor isn't the pain itself but the way we try to cope with it.

CHAPTER 5

WELCOME TO THE HUMAN CONDITION

You know it as well as I do. No one wakes up in the morning, looks in the mirror, and says, "You know what? Let me go mess up my life today!" Even though that's never our goal, it doesn't stop us from doing things that chip away at our momentum, one choice at a time. We're not trying to sabotage ourselves on purpose. Most of the time, we're just trying to cope. And we're doing it with whatever tools or habits we've picked up along the way. Those tools may have gotten us through a hard season, but they aren't actually helping us move forward anymore.

Over the years, I've leaned hard on different habits to help me cope with stress and discomfort. Sometimes they helped. Other times they made things worse. One of the patterns I've noticed in my life is how much harder everything feels at night. During the day, I'm moving. I have work to accomplish, calls to make, and goals to chase. But when the world quiets down, that's when my overthinking brain kicks things into overdrive. This is called RNT, or repetitive negative thinking. It's when our brain runs through scenarios or thoughts over and over. There's an actual neurological reason for that.

When we aren't focused on a task, our brain switches to the default mode network (DMN). This is the part of the brain that is responsible for internal dialogue, self-reflection, and mental wandering. It is directly tied to rumination and worry.

Pair that with our natural circadian rhythms, which help our brains wind down at night, and it is not surprising that rumination and worries spike. The more we glide into our circadian rhythm, the fewer stimuli we have and the more our DMN takes over. The quiet truly does amplify everything. I've heard it said, "The mind is like a magnifying glass. When the world quiets down, thoughts get louder."[31]

> **We're not trying to sabotage ourselves on purpose. Most of the time, we're just trying to cope.**

A study by specialists in behavioral therapy found that 91.4 percent of things we worry about never actually end up happening. Within the ten-day study, 100 percent of the participants' concerns never came to fruition. After thirty days, the 91.4 percent rose. This probably won't surprise you, but the more we worry about situations out of our control, the higher the incidence of generalized depression and anxiety.[32]

There have been times when I couldn't stop replaying a stressful conversation, or I found myself ruminating on something that wasn't going right. And the only thing I could do to shut it down was to get to sleep as fast as possible. Sometimes I employed the help of sleep aids. I rationalized it by reminding myself that if I could just get a little reset with a good night's sleep, I could get back to center the next morning. I didn't always see that some of the ways I found relief from my stress were actually keeping me stuck.

If my rumination gets bad enough, sometimes a distraction technique helps, like watching something light-hearted to pull my mind in a different direction. As of the writing of this book, my go-to is Dry Bar Comedy. It's clean, funny stand-up that doesn't add more stress to my system. Nate Bargatze, Leanne Morgan, and Brad Upton are some of my current favorites. Their humor is smart, relatable, and just enough to give my mind a break. It might not solve the issue, but sometimes that pause gives me just enough space to breathe and reset.

My turning point came when I started realizing that numbing out, whether it was with food, distractions, or even work tasks, wasn't fixing anything. It was like running miles on a treadmill in the basement and then turning it off, only to realize I was still in the same room and nothing had changed. I'd have a brief moment of comfort, and then the same weight of the world was right there waiting for me.

I began to see that the real antidote to anxiety wasn't escape. It was action. More than that, it was consistent action. One win led to another. One good decision fueled the next. This should all sound familiar by now. That's how momentum works because it's self-generating. When I could finally see where I wanted to go and had the confidence to believe in myself, my momentum began to shift in the right direction.

> **I began to see that the real antidote to anxiety wasn't escape. It was action.**

It isn't just something I felt. It lines up with what psychology teaches about anxiety. Avoidance and escape might give temporary relief, but they can also reinforce the fear underneath. Proactive, purposeful action creates a sense of control. It builds mastery and helps us solve the problems we're tempted to run from. That's the heart of cognitive-behavioral therapy: don't avoid, lean in. Walk through it, and you'll make lasting changes.[33]

That's not just true in business. It's true in every area of life. I've seen it in my career in the mortgage world. The results of today's efforts may not show up immediately, but I've been doing this long enough to know the process works. I just have to keep showing up.

I've seen it in my personal health journey too. For years I carried around extra weight and told myself from time to time that I'd get serious about it "someday."

But someday didn't exist until the reason I needed to do something became louder than my excuses. For me, that wake-up call came in the form of a colonoscopy that revealed four polyps and a diagnosis of non-alcoholic fatty liver disease. That was my line-in-the-sand moment. And I stayed with it.

I didn't completely overhaul everything overnight. At first, I couldn't find the discipline I thought I needed to lose weight, and that's why I kept falling off the wagon. It wasn't until I jump-started my weight loss journey with the help of my obesity medical physician that I was able to make lasting changes. Now, with the help of my doctor and my dietitian, I'm more intentional about what I am putting in my body, and I can keep the weight off and feel better.

I started small: cutting out snacks after 7:00 p.m., drinking more water, and walking two to three miles a day. Not running, walking. Not hitting the gym like a maniac. Just walking. Consistently. And that's what made the difference. I had to find something I could stick with. And eventually, it worked. I lost forty pounds. Consistency really is key. And so is finding professionals who can help when you can't seem to figure something out on your own.

SELF-SABOTAGE HIDES IN PLAIN SIGHT

Most of us already know the habits that hold us back: late-night scrolling, the extra drink, the avoidance of a difficult conversation or phone call. We tell ourselves we're just taking a little break, just watching one more show, or just rewarding ourselves after a long day. But here's the truth: These little habits may seem harmless, but they're the very things that keep us stuck.

Self-sabotage isn't always dramatic. It can look like productivity. Maybe instead of writing the next chapter, we can reorganize the desk. It disguises itself as self-care when we allow ourselves to eat some comfort food instead of exercising. It may call itself motivational when we read five self-help books in a row without implementing a single idea into our everyday lives.

Self-sabotaging behaviors mimic progress. Remember the illusion of momentum from Chapter 3? We are tricking ourselves into thinking we're doing something. But what we're actually doing is avoiding discomfort. And avoidance is expensive.

We don't sabotage ourselves because we're lazy. We do it because we're in pain, and we haven't processed it.

Whether it's anxiety, insecurity, loneliness, or shame, the real trigger behind destructive behaviors is emotional discomfort. We avoid hard things because we don't want to feel the feelings they bring up, and we reach for a coping mechanism instead. And as long as we never ask ourselves why, we'll keep repeating the same cycle.

So how can self-sabotage show up in our lives?

Let's start with procrastination. At first glance, it may seem like laziness. But it's actually fear. We delay the hard task ahead of us not because we don't care but because starting it means facing uncertainty or potential failure. As a mortgage originator, I've seen this firsthand. Mortgage lenders don't put off prospecting for sales because they lack time or the knowledge of what to say. They put it off because they're afraid of rejection on that call. That fear turns into call reluctance, and it's one of the biggest momentum killers in sales.

Next is distraction. In this digital age, distraction is a constant companion, just one swipe away. Whether it's social media or streaming, these platforms are engineered for dopamine hits. There have been studies using functional MRI that show positive feedback in our brains when we interact with likes, comments, and shares that make us feel good. Over time, those dopamine hits from social media can keep us from being present. We stop thinking, and we stop growing. Distraction can steal our focus and erode our potential, one minute at a time.[34]

Another way to sabotage our momentum is by self-medicating. Self-medication goes deeper than most of us realize. It isn't just drugs or alcohol, although those are the most destructive. It's also food, porn, endless entertainment, or even obsessive reading about self-improvement. It's anything we use to avoid being with our emotions. And until we identify the pain we're actually trying to numb or avoid and the trigger that turned our focus away from our momentum, we'll keep running.

What I've found ironic in my life is that sometimes what looks like growth is actually a cleverly disguised escape. I've always been interested in how the human mind works. I have a psychology degree, so part of this runs deep for me. I'm wired to ask why we do what we do.

There were times when I would dive into personal growth books, not so much to grow but to avoid. I'd read to escape the emotional pain I was feeling, especially during seasons where life wasn't moving the way I hoped. And it looked good from the outside. No one questioned me about it. I was learning. But I wasn't doing the work I should have been doing.

Deep down, I was hoping to find a quick fix. Sometimes the books helped. They gave me language to describe what I was experiencing and tools to manage my emotions, and to hope. Other times, they simply distracted me from facing what I needed to feel.

Self-sabotaging behaviors feel good in the moment. They can reduce our discomfort and give us a sense of control. But it's an illusion. It's fake productivity and temporary relief instead of long-term healing, and the cost is massive when it comes to our momentum.

Every time you set a task or goal, you're not just making a plan. You're making a promise to yourself. When you consistently don't follow through, your inner system starts keeping score. Not loudly. Subtly. The message that seeps in isn't "I failed at this task" but "I don't keep my word to myself." Over time, that erodes self-trust. And once self-trust takes a hit, motivation doesn't disappear; it stops showing up on command. Your brain learns, "We talk a big game, but we don't act." So it stops lending you energy.

The real risk isn't the unfinished task. It's the identity drift that follows. Miss enough self-set commitments and you start lowering the bar without realizing it. You set softer goals, avoid deadlines, and delay starts because part of you already expects the letdown. That's how a bad day quietly becomes a pattern. Momentum doesn't die from one miss; it dies from repeated, unexamined misses that train you to hesitate.

The fix isn't to try harder. It's to set smaller, cleaner promises and keep them. Under-promise. Over-execute. Make your goals behavior-based and finishable, not aspirational and vague. Completing a small task restores credibility with yourself. Each follow-through deposits trust back into the account.

It's like we train our brains to expect failure or inconsistency. And when that narrative loops long enough, we stop trusting ourselves or stop trying altogether. That's why the small promises we keep to ourselves matter so much. Every time we follow through, even in the smallest way, we're reinforcing a new identity that says, "I can be counted on, even by me."

Your internal view of yourself sets the boundaries for what you believe is possible. And believing you can change is what makes that change possible.

LESSONS LEARNED

When it comes to breaking free from destructive behavioral patterns, I haven't always gotten it right. I've fallen into the same traps we're talking about: numbing, self-sabotaging, choosing comfort over growth, and escaping through distraction instead of facing what hurts. And it has happened more than once. I'm still a work in progress. Isn't that part of the human condition for all of us?

We all have these automatic behavior loops that can take over when our energy tanks are running low. It's easy to shame ourselves into believing that the answer lies in our ability to have willpower or discipline, but I've learned that it goes deeper than that. We first have to consciously see our patterns, and that takes self-awareness.

Sometimes we're the ones who notice the behavior is destructive. Other times we hear it from a friend or family member who points it out. Either way, when the moment of recognition comes, the worst thing we can do is pile on shame or judgment. And yet that's often where we go first. It's natural to feel those things. But what I've noticed is this: Recognizing a pattern requires honesty, curiosity, and even a little grace and compassion for ourselves.

A huge turning point for me came when I stopped asking, "Why can't I stop doing this?" and started asking, "What purpose is this serving in my life?" Because every form of self-sabotage has a hidden benefit. It gives us comfort. It helps us avoid risk. It gives us back a little sense of control when life feels too big or painful. That doesn't mean it's good for us, but it does mean we need to understand the *why* before we try to change the *what*.

I've learned that many of my own self-destructive behaviors were rooted in unmet needs or unaddressed pain: overeating at night, doom scrolling, impulsive online shopping, and ruminating in bed as I catastrophized worst-case scenarios until 3:00 a.m. I can't tell you how many online purchases I've made late at night that I ended up returning in the morning, wondering, "What was I thinking?"

Here's the thing: I didn't have to think. Algorithms track everything we do on different platforms—posts we like, comments we leave, ads we click, how long we spend viewing certain types of posts—and then it just keeps giving us more of what we like.

We're most vulnerable to those unhealthy coping mechanisms when our energy is depleted and our guard is down. I still struggle with late-night snacking, especially during stressful seasons. I still catch myself reaching for the quick dopamine hit instead of the deeper healing I really need. But I've learned some practical tools that help interrupt those patterns. I'm passionate about passing them along as someone who knows what it feels like to be stuck and wants you to know you're not alone.

One of the most helpful tools I've used is something I call the five-minute delay rule. When the urge hits to scroll, snack, shop, or spiral, I give myself five minutes to redirect my attention. I read a few pages of a book. I get up and change my environment. I send a text to a friend or family member, or I say something out loud that interrupts the thought loop. More often than not, by the end of those five minutes, the urge has passed.

This isn't just some personal hack; neuroscience backs it up. Judson Brewer, a neuroscientist and addiction psychiatrist, talks about this in his book *The Craving Mind.* His research shows that mindfulness actually helps interrupt the automatic loops that drive destructive behavior.

When we create even a short pause, we begin to rewire the brain's reward system.[35]

Making small environmental changes is also helpful. For example, I've deleted apps or moved them off my home screen so they're not the first thing I see. I know social media can be useful for our work and staying connected, but I don't want it to be the first place I go when I wake up. I've also changed my physical location when I feel stuck in a loop. Just stepping into a different room or going for a walk can disrupt the cycle.

Sometimes it's better to focus on a replacement behavior instead of what you don't want to do. In his book *Tiny Habits*, behavioral scientist BJ Fogg talks about using anchor moments to build new routines.[36] Rather than trying to change everything all at once or relying on sheer discipline, we can tie a small, positive action to a regular part of our day, and that habit naturally starts to grow. I've started anchoring certain negative behaviors that weren't serving me anymore to phrases like "I'm not that person anymore." That simple identity statement helps me remember who I want to be. Like James Clear says in *Atomic Habits,* "Every action you take is a vote for the type of person you want to become."[37] We're combining an identity change with a behavior change.

Even with these tools, I still mess up now and then. That's where grace comes in. I used to think that success meant getting it perfect every time. But it turns out the opposite is true. In her book *Grit,* Angela Duckworth explains that long-term success is less about flawless performance and more about how we respond when we inevitably fail. That's where the concept of a failure routine comes into play.[38]

She doesn't hand us a single checklist; she shows us what it looks like in real life. People with grit don't just bounce back from failure; they have a repeatable way of doing it. They acknowledge the setback without letting it define them. They step back, analyze what went wrong, and then adjust their game plan. Most importantly, they don't quit. They persist with renewed focus because they've trained themselves to see failure as specific and temporary rather than a reflection of who they are.

That's the habit I've been trying to build. When I stumble, instead of spiraling into shame or giving up, I remind myself that this is part of the process. Failure is just a cue to recommit.

Sometimes connecting to a deeper purpose works. Viktor Frankl—Austrian psychiatrist, Holocaust survivor, and author of *Man's Search for Meaning*—wrote, "Those who have a clear why can endure almost any how."[39] His perspective wasn't just theoretical; it was created through unthinkable suffering in Nazi concentration camps where he observed that those who found meaning were the ones most likely to survive.

Self-sabotage isn't always dramatic. It can look like productivity.

That's been true in my life. When I can tie my actions to something bigger than myself, I find it easier to stick with the behaviors that build momentum. I'm not just resisting a destructive behavior; I'm leaning toward something that matters.

A deeper purpose also helps when I feel tempted to isolate myself. Depending on the time of day, I will go to the local coffee shop or bookstore to be around other people. I love to meet people and have interesting conversations with strangers. One of the biggest lies that keeps us stuck in destructive behavior is the belief that we're alone in it. That no one would understand. That we have to figure it out on our own. But we don't. And we shouldn't. Sometimes we need to ask for help. Whether it's a coach, counselor, friend, or support group, just saying "I'm struggling" can be the first step toward a momentum shift.

Keep in mind, if you see yourself in anything I've shared here, take a breath. You aren't broken. You're human. The fact that you're even reading this means you're already open to making little changes that have a huge impact on your momentum.

TAKE RESPONSIBILITY

It's time to talk about something that can be difficult to admit. Sometimes we know we're not making the right choice, and we do it anyway. We tell ourselves we deserve it, we're tired, or it's harmless. But if we're being honest, it isn't harmless. We're hiding or checking out. And over time, it can cost us our momentum.

In the movie *The Legend of Bagger Vance,* Bagger Vance isn't just a caddie who shows up at the right time. He becomes a guide and coach to a golfer in desperate need of healing. With his tough love and no-nonsense approach, Bagger helps Rannulph Junuh remember the man he used to be before the trauma of war threatened to leave him broken.

Junuh comes home from the war physically alive but spiritually collapsed. He used to be a hero, a golf prodigy, and a name people spoke about with pride in their eyes. But trauma stripped away his identity. And like so many of us, he didn't know how to come back. So he drank, kept to himself, and let his life get small. He wallowed in self-pity.

Hear me when I say he wasn't weak; he was wounded. The turning point has an interesting twist. Junuh doesn't find freedom when Bagger Vance shows up with all the answers. He finds it when he accepts the truth, stops running from his pain, and chooses to get back into the game.

That's what taking responsibility looks like. It has nothing to do with blame, shame, or self-punishment, and everything to do with making the quiet decision to stop outsourcing our momentum to our circumstances. We

You aren't broken. You're human.

don't need to wait for life to get easier before we show up again. We don't need to wait for more time, energy, or support before we take our next step.

Taking responsibility means saying, "I might not have caused my pain, but I'm in charge of my healing." We have the ability to stop living at the mercy of our lowest moments and start remembering who we were before our circumstances tried to convince us to shrink.

Most people think of responsibility as a burden. I see it as the beginning of freedom. When you take responsibility, you aren't powerless. The truth is that self-sabotaging behavior doesn't define us. It reveals something. It's a signal, not a life sentence.

Take self-pity. We've all had it at one point or another. It can feel good temporarily because it provides an emotional release, validation, and sense of comfort, but this relief is often deceptive and short-lived.

> **The truth is that self-sabotaging behavior doesn't define us. It reveals something. It's a signal, not a life sentence.**

Science backs this up. Our brains aren't wired for infinite willpower. We're wired to conserve energy. When we're exhausted, overwhelmed, or emotionally raw, the brain's default is to choose whatever brings short-term relief. It's simple biology. But here's the part we don't always want to hear: Knowing that doesn't give us an excuse to stay stuck.[40]

Understanding the brain's limits should breed self-compassion, yes. But it should also spark your responsibility. Because the moment you understand what's happening, you can't pretend you're just a victim of your habits.

Junuh had every reason to stay broken after he came back from the war. No one would have blamed him. But he didn't heal by isolating himself. He healed by remembering who he was and choosing to take responsibility for the outcomes in his life.

The longer we stay in survival mode, the more disconnected we become from ourselves. We might look functional on the outside, but inside, we're not present. We're performing a version of our lives instead of actually living. That's not just emotionally exhausting; it's neurologically real.

Research from neuroimaging studies shows that when we're mentally checked out—whether by ruminating, scrolling, or numbing—the default mode network (DMN) in our brain becomes activated.[41] And the more time we spend in that mode, the harder it becomes to make intentional decisions because DMN dominance disrupts the networks responsible for focus, problem-solving, and goal-directed behavior.[42] In fact, research has shown that persistent rumination, mind-wandering, and passive digital consumption all increase DMN activity while weakening the executive systems the brain relies on for clarity and action.[43]

> **Your internal view of yourself sets the boundaries for what you believe is possible. And believing you can change is what makes that change possible.**

In other words, numbing isn't neutral. It rewires our brains for passivity. It chips away at our agency. We become less likely to move, even when we know deep down that we want to. It's physics. An object at rest stays at rest.

Time management will only help us get so far. We can color-code our calendar and optimize our to-do list, but if we're running on empty, nothing sticks. We have to make the right kinds of shifts—from coping to ownership, managing time to managing energy, and checking out to checking back in.

Taking responsibility starts with understanding that energy isn't a luxury; it's a signal. It tells us what to pay attention to, protect, and replenish. We can't shame ourselves into momentum, but we can take responsibility for how we spend our energy, even when our circumstances are less than ideal.

Junuh finally does this in *The Legend of Bagger Vance*. He doesn't erase his trauma or magically feel better. He simply remembers the swing he was born with and chooses to get quiet enough to feel it again. That swing is your truest self, the part of you that was never broken, only buried.

One of the most moving moments in the movie comes near the end when Junuh is deep in the pressure of competition. He hits the ball into a tangle of trees. The shot seems impossible, and the weight of his past starts pressing in. He begins to sweat, doubt himself, and freeze. That's when Bagger says, "You ain't alone in that. But you been carryin' this one long enough. Time to go on. Lay it down."

Junuh admits, "I don't know how."

And Bagger responds with the line that gives me chills. "You got a choice. You can stop. Or you can start. . . . Now is the time. Let yourself remember. Remember your swing."[44]

That scene is applicable beyond the game of golf. We all carry burdens. The human condition is messy, and we all make mistakes. But those mistakes don't have to define us. We are not our worst moments. When we allow ourselves to get quiet, we can hear the truth again. We can remember who we are and why we're here. The swing was never gone; it was just waiting to be remembered.

We're not talking about a perfect existence or an immediate, unwavering drive to always make the right decisions. It's just one bold moment of taking responsibility.

Taking responsibility is making the decision to stop avoiding those parts of ourselves—to stop numbing what we need to face, outsourcing our futures for fatigue, or waiting for permission to begin again. We don't need to climb the entire mountain today. We just need to say, "This matters, and I'm done pretending it doesn't."

This is the choice in front of each of us. We're not talking about a perfect existence or an immediate, unwavering drive to always make the right decisions. It's just one bold moment of taking responsibility. No one can take that step for us. But the moment we do, we'll feel the shift.

ACT LIKE YOUR TWO-YEAR-OLD SELF

Have you ever been around a toddler who's in that "why" phase? It's exhausting. Your answer is barely out of your mouth, and they're at it again, "Yeah, but why?" With older children, we'll sometimes say, "Because I said so." But that answer isn't good enough for them. They will still just double down. "Why?" It can drive parents nuts, but maybe toddlers are onto something. Maybe the problem with how we've been approaching our own growth is that we stop asking too soon.

That's the spirit I've tried to bring into this chapter, even as I wrestled with it myself. When I started writing about self-sabotage, distractions, and coping mechanisms, I kept hitting walls. I knew these weren't just surface-level issues. They're layered and rooted. And I found myself circling the same question over and over again: "But why?"

Why do we default to the things that drain us? Why do we wait until our bodies are screaming before we rest? Why do we reach for our vices before we ever pause to just rest?

These questions don't have clean answers, but they do have patterns. And identifying our patterns is where we can begin to make lasting changes.

One of the first major shifts came from Tony Schwartz and his work on energy management. Most of us live as if time is the issue. We never have enough hours in a day, right? But what Schwartz helped me see is that we should stop focusing on hours and start recognizing our energy.

Our best contributions don't come from time on the clock; they come from our sustained, focused energy. That's when I started paying attention to what I was doing, but more importantly to when I had the energy to do it well. Then I looked at why I felt so depleted in the first place.[45]

Then there's James Clear, whose work on habits is deceptively simple but widely effective. He taught me that your life doesn't rise to the level of your goals. It falls to the level of your routines. That hit me hard. I had all these great intentions, but I kept falling into the same ruts because I didn't change the system underneath. I was trying to will my way out of deeply ingrained patterns without examining the cues that were triggering them. And once I started asking, "*Why* does this keep happening?" I realized that every behavior was my body trying to solve something. My habits were meeting my needs. So I had to learn how to meet that need in a better way.[46]

Mel Robbins gave me a tool that was so simple that I almost didn't take it seriously at first: the five-second rule. But I'm living proof that it works. When you feel yourself start to spiral or when you're hesitating, count down from five and just move. The science shows that it interrupts the autopilot response and gives your prefrontal cortex a chance to reengage. But what it really did for me was create a tiny space between impulse and action. It gave me a doorway out of the loop. Because again, I asked, "*Why* do I let these patterns run the show?" And Robbins helped me see that even a five-second pause can be the beginning of a healthier habit.[47]

Then I ran across Jill Bolte Taylor, a neuroscientist who went through a stroke and wrote about how our emotions only last for ninety seconds in the body unless we feed them. That blew my mind. Ninety seconds. That's it. I had been dragging around emotional states for days, weeks, and even months, thinking they were just permanent parts of me at that point. But no, those feelings were meant to pass. I was the one choosing to replay them on a loop. And again, I had to stop and ask, "*Why? Why* do I keep stoking emotions that aren't serving me? What am I getting from it? What's it protecting me from? What's it distracting me from doing?"[48]

And as I kept digging, I found a quote that is now engraved on my brain. Viktor Frankl was attributed as saying, "Between stimulus and response there is a space. In that space is our power to choose our response." Fighting for that space means slowing down long enough to see the pattern. It means asking better questions, not moving on from the moment too fast. It means becoming like that little two-year-old: stubborn, relentless, and unwilling to accept the first answer. Ever.

I know asking *why* sounds simple, but if you keep pulling on that thread, it will take you somewhere deeper. If you can take inventory of where your momentum gets derailed, you can start to treat the reasons with more honesty and self-compassion. Try the following action steps to help you create new awareness that can help you build patterns to move you into action.

Identify your go-to escape routes. This first step is brutally simple, but it works: Track your day—not in a perfectionist, time-blocked, hustle-culture kind of way. I'm talking about a raw, honest, pen-to-paper audit of where your time and energy go.

What do you do from the moment you wake up to the moment your head hits the pillow? Write it down. Yes, all of it. The meetings and the emails, sure. But also the hour-long rabbit-hole dive you took on social media, the late-night ice cream, the "just one episode" that turned into four.

It's like what my doctor told me when I had gut issues: "Write down everything you eat. Everything. Even the M&Ms." She wasn't trying to shame me; she was trying to help me see what I couldn't. Same goes here. We're working on awareness, not judgment.

If you're honest for even just three to five days, patterns will emerge. And from there, you can ask better questions. When do I feel most tempted to check out, overeat, scroll, or drink? What emotions usually come up right before I distract myself? What three behaviors do I use the most to self-soothe or escape?

This isn't easy, but it's powerful. If you can finally see it, you can shift it.

Dr. Judson Brewer talks about this in his book *Unwinding Anxiety.* He says that when we bring curiosity and awareness to our habits, we interrupt their automatic grip. Taking a look at what we do each day can help us see which habits we'd like to outgrow.[49]

Connect the trigger to the escape. After you've identified your most common destructive behaviors, the next step is to dig into the *why* behind them. Remember, it isn't enough to say "I procrastinate" or "I eat when I'm stressed." You have to become the two-year-old again. *Why?* What triggered that need to escape? What emotion came right before it?

Here's an example from my own life.

Trigger: Feeling overwhelmed at work
Escape: A big bowl of Blue Bell ice cream
Relief: Temporary distraction with a sugary treat
Cost: Adding inches to my waistline

That's a pattern I've repeated too many times. Short-term relief always comes with a long-term cost. Every destructive behavior offers something in the moment, but it also robs us of something meaningful over time, whether it's sleep, creativity, confidence, or connection.

When my boys were little, we were hooked on the game *Plants vs. Zombies*. Another time, it was *Clash Royale*. These games are designed with bright colors, constant dopamine hits, and micro-rewards to keep you playing. I wasn't sleeping. I wasn't reading. I wasn't learning. When I finally deleted them, I realized I'd also spent real money inside those apps. It wasn't a lot in my case since I am stingy, but one study showed the top *Clash of Clans* player spent $12,000. And another person spent $30,000 across both *Clash of Clans* and *Clash Royale*. You can't even begin to calculate the opportunity cost.[50]

I deleted all games from my phone because I wasn't stewarding my energy and time the way I wanted to. It was hurting my momentum.

Experiment with energy management. One of the biggest mindset shifts I've made is this: You don't have a time management problem; you have an energy management problem. Let me explain.

When I first started tracking my day, I noticed something weird. I had plenty of hours to get things done, but my energy was a different story. I'd hit a wall at 2:00 p.m. and then crash again at 9:00 p.m. So I started tracking what I was doing along with how I felt while doing it—energized, drained, focused, or fuzzy. That's when things started to click.

In their book *The Power of Full Engagement*, Jim Loehr and Tony Schwartz write, "Energy, not time, is the fundamental currency of high performance. . . Performance, health, and happiness are grounded in the skillful management of energy."[51]

I started designing my day based on three energy zones:

High-energy window – do deep, creative, strategic work

Mid-energy window – handle meetings, feedback, and training

Low-energy window – knock out admin tasks, emails, and errands

This is called task-energy alignment, and it's a game-changer.

Take some time to reflect on your energy throughout the day, and see what happens when you match the type of work you do with the energy you have to do it.

Congratulations on deciding to start asking yourself *why* you do the things you do. As you continue to identify and replace those self-sabotaging behaviors, it's time to keep the momentum going.

CHAPTER 6

EMBRACE FULFILLMENT ON YOUR OWN TERMS

I don't think I ever consciously set out to chase someone else's definition of success. But I did chase something. For a long time, I was going after what society told me would make me feel like I mattered: money, awards, titles, and status. That's what we're all taught, right? That success looks like a number in a bank account, a line on a résumé, or a parking space with your name on it.

And I bought into it.

I remember hitting one of my biggest income goals and thinking, *Okay, this is it. I've arrived.* But I hadn't. I hit the goal, and the celebration was short-lived. The next morning, I woke up and asked myself, *Now what?* I thought I would feel a sense of completion, like the fulfill-ment switch would flip on and everything would just click.

But it didn't. If anything, it stirred up even more questions.

That's when I started realizing something I hadn't been willing to admit before: Chasing goals without exam-ining the *why* behind them always leaves you a little empty and low on momen-tum to keep going. I wasn't chasing my best self. I was chasing benchmarks that didn't actually mean any-thing to me. And the crazy part was that I wasn't unhappy. I just wasn't fulfilled.

Chasing goals without examining the why behind them always leaves you a little empty and low on momentum to keep going.

There's a difference.

I had achieved a level of success that looked great from the outside, but inside, I felt like I was circling something I couldn't fully define.

One of the biggest shifts for me came during a season of early fatherhood. At that time, I loved to golf. It was my way of releasing stress and creating a mental reset. But with little kids at home, my golf time slowed down and began to disappear altogether. I remember talking to a retired friend who said something that stuck with me. He told me, "There's a time and a season for everything."

For him, retirement meant morning tee times and walks with old friends. And I envied that freedom. But he wasn't saying I should be doing what he was doing. He was reminding me that fulfillment changes depending on the season of life we're in.

That conversation planted a seed for me. It gave me permission to define fulfillment on my own terms, not as something static or fixed but as something fluid and tied more to who I wanted to become than what I wanted to collect. For a while, I wrestled with this question: *Is it wrong to keep chasing something?* I've always had a growth mindset. I like setting goals. I enjoy pushing my own limits. But what I've learned is that growth in and of itself doesn't equal fulfillment.

Fulfillment changes depending on the season of life we're in.

Balance becomes the soil, and fulfillment grows in it.

Without balance, there's no room for presence, and fulfillment can't survive without it. We can't feel deeply fulfilled if we're constantly rushed, fractured, and fried. Balance, in a way, is the delivery system that helps fulfillment get through to us.

I've seen this pattern show up time and again in my own life and in the people around me. Imagine someone who is crushing it at work, hitting all the sales goals, and climbing the ladder. But their marriage is hanging by a thread, their health is on the back burner, and their hobbies have become "What hobbies?"

On paper, it looks like success, but in their soul, there's a void. They're out of balance. And without balance, fulfillment fades because wholeness is missing. And that's what fulfillment really is: a sense of integration between who we are, what we value, and how we're showing up in our daily lives.

It isn't something we can fake. We can't brute-force our way into fulfillment. We can't schedule our way into it. We have to be present enough to recognize what matters and aligned enough to build our lives around that.

Balance allows us to bring our full selves to the table. Our body, mind, relationships, and spirit all get to have a seat. And when they're not constantly fighting for scraps of our attention, something powerful happens. We begin to feel like we're living from the inside out, not the outside in.

The question I keep coming back to is this: *What's the motivation behind the chase?* Is it rooted in purpose and becoming more of who I was created to be, or is it driven by insecurity, comparison, or ego?

That distinction matters. It's the difference between chasing something because it looks good on paper and pursuing something that aligns with our core values. When we're honest with ourselves, we can usually tell the difference.

You can have a growth mindset and be fulfilled at the same time. You can want to do more, serve more, and create more without getting trapped in the cycle of never having enough. But you can't skip the hard questions: *What matters most to me? What does success actually feel like? Am I chasing something that fuels my soul or just my social media feed?*

WHEN LIFE FEELS EMPTY

There's a tension that quietly builds in all of us when our behaviors don't align with our values. We say we want to treat our bodies like temples, love our spouses the way they deserve to be loved, and never speak poorly of others, to name just a few.

But when no one's watching, what are we really doing?

John Wooden said it best: "The true test of a man's character is what he does when no one is watching."

It starts with honesty with ourselves. If we cannot be honest with ourselves, then reaching fulfillment will be almost impossible. As Michael Jackson suggests in his song from the 1980s, each of us needs to take a look at the man in the mirror.

Often when I look at my life and I am not feeling fulfilled, it's because I'm not being honest with myself. My actions are out of alignment with my ideals or values.

We often care about what others see, so we show ourselves to the public in the way we want to be seen. But who are we *really*? This is so common in what we see on social media. But who are we in private? What do our actions in private show? Those actions in public need to align with our actions in private. Tony Robbins said, "You are rewarded in public for what you practice in private."[52]

I'm not trying to lay a guilt trip on you. Those are some honest questions worth asking ourselves. Because the bigger the gap between who we want to be and who we are, the heavier life seems. And the heavier life seems, the less fulfilled we feel.

I've felt that gap. During the seasons of my life when I was most out of sync, it was because my actions consistently fell below my values. And when that becomes your baseline, no amount of accomplishment can fill the void. You look in the mirror, and some unnamed thing feels off. We all want to believe we're living with purpose, but too often we're just performing.

That disconnect gets even more complex in a culture like ours where fulfillment is often measured by individual achievement. The Western world tends to reward self-made success in the form of increased wealth, greater social influence, and more personal accolades. But when I spent two years in Argentina when I was nineteen and twenty years old, I saw something radically different. Families of four living in tiny homes with barely enough food in the fridge appeared more fulfilled than people I knew back home who had everything money could buy. Their sense of success came from community, shared meals, and purpose—from a life lived together. They valued belonging with one another over accumulating things. And that changed my understanding of fulfillment.

You cannot build momentum by looking sideways.

We're bombarded with the message that we're only as valuable as our next achievement. With that mindset, it's easy to fall into the trap of constantly moving the goalpost.

We set a goal, hit it, and then what? Instead of celebrating, we raise the bar, compare ourselves to the next level, or start to chase what someone else has.

But whose life are we trying to build—our authentic life or the one we think we should want?

That's where comparison creeps in. And it's sneaky. It shifts with every stage of life. In college, we compare ourselves to our classmates. A decade later, we're comparing salaries, homes, kids, and platforms. We upgrade our peer groups, and added pressure comes with the next level. It's a never-ending cycle because the benchmark is always external. We hardly ever ask ourselves, "What fulfills me?" Instead, it's usually, "How do I measure up?"

Theodore Roosevelt is attributed as saying, "Comparison is the thief of joy." We can add that comparison is also the thief of fulfillment. When it comes to comparison, I love what Steven Furtick wrote in his book *Crash the Chatterbox*: "The reason we struggle with insecurity is that we compare our behind-the-scenes with everyone else's highlight reel."[53]

You cannot build momentum by looking sideways. When you get distracted by comparison, it's like taking your foot off the gas pedal and your eyes off the road. Every minute you are comparing, you are not creating your best, authentic self. Success isn't being ahead of someone else. It's being aligned with you. If you want fulfillment, stop running someone else's race.

This isn't just about emotional frustration; it's biological. Our brains are wired to notice what we're exposed to. Buy a new, red Honda CR-V, and suddenly we see red Honda CR-Vs everywhere. Learn a new word, and it pops up in every conversation. That's not a coincidence; it's the Baader-Meinhof phenomenon, also known as *frequency illusion*. And it's deeply connected to how the brain's reticular activating system (RAS) works.

Your RAS acts like a mental filter, scanning the world for information that confirms what you've decided matters. The Baader-Meinhof phenomenon proves your brain isn't just a processor; it's a pattern detector. Once a thought becomes significant to you, your brain makes it visible. You don't see more red CR-Vs because there are more of them. You see them because your brain decided they're worth noticing. And that's exactly what happens with comparison.[54]

If we're constantly consuming content that tells us what success should look like, how we should dress, where we should be by now, and what we should have accomplished, our RAS locks in on that. It turns social scrolling into a subconscious scoreboard. We start measuring our lives not by what we value but by what we've been exposed to. We stop seeing progress and start obsessing over the gap. It's exhausting.

Burnout begins here—not just physical exhaustion but a deeper, soul-level fatigue— because we start chasing outcomes that never really mattered to us in the first place. We climb ladders that are leaned against walls we never wanted to be near. And eventually, we feel hollow. From the outside we might look like we're winning, but inside we feel spiritually bankrupt.

Clarity around your values is imperative. If you've never defined what fulfillment means to you, your brain will borrow a definition from the world around you. It will start chasing louder metrics such as likes, numbers, job titles, and someone else's highlight reel. You'll end up running hard in a direction that leads you farther from yourself. One day, you'll look back and wonder how you got so lost.

Fulfillment isn't a destination. It's not a title, a dollar amount, or a dream job. It's the alignment between who you are, what you value, and how you live. The wider the gap between those things, the more frustration, confusion, and disconnection you'll feel. But when those three areas come into alignment, fulfillment shows up at a deep and steady peace.

That's what happens in the tension of life. It throws curveballs, distractions, and expectations our way. How we respond reveals what we're truly anchored in. We can't control the chaos, but we can control our filter. We can choose what our minds lock onto. We can teach our brain to stop scanning for what we lack and start tuning in to what truly matters.

So the real question becomes this: Are you building a life that looks successful from the outside or one that actually feels fulfilling from within? The answer starts with what you've told your brain to see.

SUCCESS, HAPPINESS, AND FULFILLMENT

There's an important distinction between success and fulfillment that often gets blurred. And when you add happiness to the mix, it gets even more confusing. But getting clear on these differences matters, because if you don't, you might end up chasing things that were never meant to satisfy you in the first place.

Let's start with happiness. Happiness is often a momentary emotion. It's a quick high after good news, a fun trip, a great meal, or getting something you've been waiting for. Think of it like a sugar rush—bright, exciting, and fleeting. You can be happy without being fulfilled. But you can't be truly fulfilled without experiencing a deeper kind of happiness, the kind that doesn't come from a dopamine spike but from alignment with purpose.

In our family, we raise guide dogs for Guiding Eyes for the Blind. At any given time, we've usually got a puppy running around the house. They're playful, full of energy, and a whole lot of work, but we love their presence. We raise them from about two months to eighteen months old before they go to New York for their next phase of training. Watching a puppy chase its tail is one of those moments that always makes me laugh. At first, they're full of excitement. They're going in circles, all in on the chase. But then they get dizzy. They tire themselves out without actually getting anywhere.

That image has stuck with me because it's a perfect metaphor for chasing external success without grounding it in internal fulfillment.

Success tends to be external. It's shaped by benchmarks, achievements, and other people's recognition. You can often measure it: the job title, the bank account, the number of followers, the size of the house. And to be clear, there's nothing wrong with any of that. Many coaches will tell you that success requires a team, a support system, and the right timing. And I agree. Success in business, sports, or leadership rarely happens in isolation. There are systems, strategies, and communities that support it.

But fulfillment is different. Fulfillment feels more like a solo mission. It's deeply personal. It's when you're living in alignment with your goals and your values, not just what looks good on paper but what actually feels right to your soul. It's an internal mindset built over time by being consciously aware of who you are and knowing what is important to you.

That's why fulfillment can shift as we grow. What looked like success in our twenties—the grind, the hustle, the status—can feel hollow later in life if it wasn't connected to meaning. But with time and experience, fulfillment becomes something richer—a deep peace, a quiet confidence, and the sense that your life reflects who you really are.

And here's the paradox. When fulfillment, not success, becomes your true north, you actually experience a more lasting kind of happiness. It's not the puppy-tail chase or the sugar high. It's something grounded. Steady. Soul-deep.

That's the shift we all need and the distinction that changes everything.

WHAT'S YOUR DEFINITION OF FULFILLMENT?

We spend too much time chasing fulfillment as it is defined by outside influences, whether that's our culture, social media, family expectations, or our own outdated definitions of success. We see what someone else calls "the dream" and think that dream should be ours too. But real fulfillment doesn't come from adopting someone else's vision. It starts with asking the hard, clarifying question: *What does fulfillment look like for me?*

Let's slow this down and get specific because "values" is a word that gets thrown around a lot. When I say *values*, I don't mean some list of virtues written on a classroom poster. What do you actually value? What are the things in your life that would feel like a loss of purpose or identity if they were stripped away?

That list is different for everyone—and that's the point. What I define as success and fulfillment may look completely different from what someone else sees as their highest ideal.

Take my own life as an example. My wife and I view structure in radically different ways. She values steady routines, clear expectations, and peace of mind. I value growth, risk, and the potential for exponential reward. I get energized by performance-based outcomes. If I produce more or bring more value to the table, I want to see that returned. She gets energized by knowing there's a plan. Neither one of us is right or wrong, but we've had to work through the tension that comes when our versions of fulfillment don't naturally align.

And that's why the real solution begins with clarity. You have to understand your values and what you value. Those sound similar, but they carry different weights. Values might include things like integrity, compassion, or honesty. But what you value might include things like time with family, creativity, financial security, health, personal growth, or impact. The more honest you are about what you value, the easier it becomes to measure your fulfillment against something real instead of something made up or handed down from a place outside of yourself.

This is what Brian Tracy points to in his book *Success Is a Journey* when he describes long-term success as the ability to identify one great goal worth pursuing and align all your efforts in that direction. He emphasized that achievement starts with clarity. And clarity becomes sustainable when it's rooted in your actual values, not just your ambition.

I love what Tracy says about building a success pattern in the subconscious mind. He writes, "When you complete a major task, overcome a great obstacle or achieve an important goal, you experience the emotions of exhilaration, joy, satisfaction, happiness, and personal pride. You set a pattern in your subconscious mind that forever after motivates you to repeat the same type of experience that leads to the same feelings."[55] That's goal-setting that also contributes to identity-shaping. Fulfillment, in that sense, is the pursuit of becoming the kind of person who keeps showing up for what matters.

Fulfillment is something you cultivate, moment by moment, choice by choice. It's deeply personal, evolving, and non-linear. You'll experience setbacks, doubts, and resistance, and still feel grounded in a meaningful path. As we've discussed in earlier chapters, the human condition is messy. Momentum isn't linear, and neither is fulfillment.

But there's a hidden danger here too: complacency—especially if you, like many people, naturally value stability. Stability is a beautiful thing, but it can turn into stagnation if we're not careful. Comfort is a human longing, but when comfort becomes our only goal, it slowly erodes our motivation. Complacency masquerades as peace, but it's actually a momentum killer. And if you're wired like I am, too much comfort can feel like suffocation.

This is why defining your own fulfillment matters so much. Your personal understanding of fulfillment becomes a guardrail against drifting through life in someone else's version of success or in a static version of your own.

As you consider your definition of fulfillment, I will leave you with a few of my favorite quotes to consider. They're reminders that fulfillment is found in living with intention.

"Strive not to be a success, but rather to be of value." This Albert Einstein quote always centers me, especially when my drive to achieve starts to eclipse my desire to serve.

Winston Churchill is attributed as saying, "Success consists of going from failure to failure without loss of enthusiasm." It serves as a reminder to the grinders that the journey isn't linear, and that's not a flaw; it's reality.

Bessie Anderson Stanley once wrote in the poem "Success" that success is laughing often, loving much, and leaving the world a bit better. It's knowing that even one life has breathed easier because you lived.[56] This is to have succeeded. This hits the soul, doesn't it? It's the epitome of fulfillment and impact.

Your behavior follows your belief. And if you define your own version of fulfillment and chase your purpose, vision, and values, then your patterns will begin to reflect that internal blueprint. This is how to train yourself to succeed in ways that actually satisfy you.

A movie that illustrates our need to find our own self-defined fulfillment is *Peaceful Warrior*. At first glance, it's a story about a gifted gymnast named Dan who seems to have it all in the form of talent, physique, trophies, and recognition. He's cocky, confident, and convinced that he's already figured life out. But all that bravado was covering something up. His life looked great on paper, but his internal life was lacking. How many times have we hit a goal, landed a win, or stood on top of some success only to feel like something's still missing?

That's the trap: external wins without internal alignment. It looks like an achievement, but it feels more like spiritual poverty.

Dan had the accolades, the skill, and the momentum, but he was still lost. His breakthrough didn't come from standing on a podium. It came after a life-altering accident when everything he identified with was stripped away. Only then did he begin to rebuild his life from the inside out.

That's what makes *Peaceful Warrior* more than just a sports drama. It's a personal development masterclass in disguise. Beneath the surface of gymnastics routines and competitive drive, it quietly delivers a deeper message: Fulfillment isn't found in applause or performance. It's built into the silent choices we make when no one's watching. It's every rep, every breath, and every decision to choose presence over proving ourselves.

> **Often when I look at my life and I am not feeling fulfilled, it's because I'm not being honest with myself. My actions are out of alignment with my ideals or values.**

There's a moment in the film when Dan realizes the fight isn't somewhere out there; it's within him. And that fight for alignment is one we all have to face. *Peaceful Warrior* is about trading ego for purpose, letting go of needing to look successful, and learning how to be whole.[57]

True fulfillment comes when you know why you're doing what you're doing and you're at peace with the person you're becoming—not someday, not when you think you've arrived, but right now, in the middle of the process. That's the invitation the movie offers: to stop chasing significance and start embodying it instead.

So how do you start?

Get practical. Make a list of your top five values. Then, next to each one, write down one way you're currently honoring that value and one way you're contradicting it. Be honest with yourself. When you can look at your life and say, "Yes, I'm becoming the person I say I want to be," that's when the momentum shifts in the right direction.

Don't expect perfection. As Harvey Mackay wrote in the foreword to Brian Tracy's book,

The great success formula has always been the same. First, decide exactly what you want and where you want to go. Second, set a deadline to make a plan to get there. Third, take action on your plan, do something every day to move toward your goal. Finally, resolve in advance that you will persist until you succeed, that you will never, ever give up.[58]

That's the mindset shift: identifying and honoring your own ideal. And when life throws challenges your way, remember this from Epictetus, the Roman philosopher, "Circumstances do not make the man, they merely reveal him to himself."[59] You're only stuck if you refuse to define success on your own terms.

Consider what Thomas Jefferson once said: "If you want something you have never had, you must be willing to do something you have never done."[60] That's the heart of fulfillment, not arriving somewhere but becoming someone, the kind of person you're proud to be because you're living from the inside out.

That journey starts now with clarity, courage, and the quiet conviction that fulfillment is never handed to you; it's built—one value-aligned choice at a time.

So again, what's your definition of fulfillment? Because until you can answer that honestly, you might spend your energy climbing the wrong mountain or running in circles like a puppy chasing its tail—dizzy but determined, without ever getting anywhere.

GAINING CLARITY

The ultimate goal is to live in a space where success and fulfillment aren't mutually exclusive. To get there, you need to do more than reflect. You need to act. The action steps below are designed to help you align what matters most to you with how you live, work, and show up in your life.

Write your eulogy. I'm not suggesting this to be morbid but so you can be honest with yourself. Take the time to find some clarity here. How do you want to be remembered? What did you achieve? How did you make people feel? How did your life reflect your values?

Write out the version of your story that you want told at your funeral. Then ask yourself how aligned it is with the way you live today. What do you need to change? And what steps can you take to make those changes?

Prioritize growth over glory. There's nothing wrong with wanting to win, but true satisfaction comes from becoming better instead of just appearing successful from the outside. Start tracking your progress in terms of who you're becoming. Ask questions like these: "Am I more patient than I was six months ago? Am I more generous, more disciplined, or more at peace? Growth isn't as flashy as glory, but it builds something that lasts.

Define value-driven goals. Anyone can set a target like "make six figures," but the power comes when you tie that goal to a purpose. Try this formula: "I want to [achieve this goal] so I can [serve this value]." For example, "I want to earn $100,000 so I can give 10 percent to causes I care about, invest in my kids' futures, and take my parents on a trip." The deeper the why, the more sustainable your momentum.

> **Fulfillment isn't a destination. It's not a title, a dollar amount, or a dream job. It's the alignment between who you are, what you value, and how you live.**

Audit your buckets. Divide your life into five categories: health, relationships, career, spirituality, and personal growth. In each category, ask yourself, "Where do I currently have momentum? Where am I coasting? Where am I stuck?"

You don't need to pour equal energy into all five at once, but you do need to stay aware of the whole picture. Momentum in one area shouldn't come at the expense of neglecting another.

Practice single-focused multitasking. Yes, that sounds counterintuitive. But hear me out. Over a month, you can tend to every aspect of life, but in any given moment, be fully present. When you're with family, be with them. When you're working, channel all your focus into the task at hand. When you're exercising, pay attention to your body.

You don't need to do everything at once. You just need to give each thing its moment. Over time, the compounding effect creates lasting alignment.

Make progress meaningful. Progress doesn't always look like a straight upward line. Consider the stock market. Zoom in, and it seems volatile. Zoom out, and you can see the trajectory. Life works the same way. Don't obsess over short-term dips in your momentum. Instead, evaluate whether your overall direction is aligned with what matters most to you. Then stay the course.

By taking these steps, you'll start aligning success with fulfillment and move toward becoming the kind of person who isn't just achieving more but is living with meaning, peace, and purpose.

CHAPTER 7

SMALL THINGS HAVE THE GREATEST IMPACT

We tend to overestimate what we can do in a year and underestimate what we can do in a decade. That's the heart of this chapter. The biggest transformations in our lives rarely begin with big, bold moves. They start with something small and repeatable that almost seems too insignificant to matter, until it does.

Take Admiral William McRaven's now-famous commencement speech at the University of Texas at Austin in 2014. He spoke to the graduating class about how to change the world, starting with one simple challenge: Make your bed, every single day.[61] It sounds pretty crazy and trivial, right? But when you think about it, repeating that one small act daily reinforces discipline, creates a quick win, and sets the tone for more wins throughout your day. His speech resonated with millions of people and became the seed of his #1 *New York Times* bestseller, *Make Your Bed: Little Things That Can Change Your Life . . . and Maybe the World.* Admiral McRaven's work reminds us of the powerful truth that small wins aren't just small. They're foundational.[62] This is one example of how easy it can be to build a morning habit. I cannot remember the last time I didn't make my bed first thing in the morning.

> **The biggest transformations in our lives rarely begin with big, bold moves.**

It's so easy to get caught up thinking that fulfillment comes from finishing the big project, hitting a massive goal, or checking off a major milestone. But it's closer to the truth to say that every big win came from a stack of smaller wins. And if we don't learn how to celebrate and repeat the small wins, we'll never build the momentum to get to the big ones.

I remember meeting with a financial planner in my twenties, shortly after my wife and I had our first child. We sat down to talk about retirement, life insurance, and long-term goals. When the planner showed how much we'd need to have to retire with the lifestyle we wanted, it was pretty overwhelming. The numbers seemed so far off that it felt impossible. But then he walked us through a set of very simple ideas: pay ourselves first, live below our means, and give time the chance to work in our favor through compounding.

That conversation helped me realize that the way to reach a big goal is by layering a series of small choices together over time. Week after week, month after month, we tracked every expense and every investment in a simple spreadsheet. It wasn't glamorous, but it gave us clarity. And with that clarity came the fuel to keep our momentum moving our finances forward. As our investments grew, slowly and surely it became more motivating to keep going. We could see that progress could happen in real time due to those small, steady steps.

Working with those spreadsheets taught me something foundational: Tracking your progress helps you see the momen-tum you're creating, because what gets measured gets managed. And what gets managed can grow.

> **Every big win came from a stack of smaller wins.**

I think about Dave Ramsey and the "debt-free screams" on his radio show. If you've never tuned in, it's the segment when people call in to announce they've paid off their debts. Most of the people aren't CEOs or specialists with six-figure salaries. They're teachers, electricians, nurses, and small business owners. They weren't lottery winners. They were everyday people who decided to make a plan and stick to it consistently. Every little payment that felt small on its own added up to financial freedom for them and their families.[63]

It's the same with our physical health. We can't lose 40 pounds in one week. We lose it one walk, one salad, and one skipped soda at a time. We can't build muscle with one gym session. We build it with reps—consistent, ordinary, unsexy reps that can change our bodies over time and, more importantly, change how we see ourselves.

BJ Fogg explains in *Tiny Habits*, "Small doesn't mean insignificant—it means strategic."[64] That one line holds a lot of power. We need to shift our minds from equating small with weak and instead start seeing small as sustainable. In a world that constantly pushes us to go big or go home, the real wins actually come from going small and staying steady.

If you've ever tried to take on too much at once, you've felt this firsthand. I've made big bets that looked great on the surface but didn't pan out. I jumped into opportunities that sounded like shortcuts to success, only to realize I skipped over the foundation I needed to make it work. Slow and steady really does win the race.

Momentum won't show up in your life fully formed.

So here's where I want to begin this chapter—not with hype, but with humility. You don't need to overhaul your whole life this week. You just need to win one small battle today. Make the bed, do the pushup, send the thank-you text, and then celebrate that first win.

Momentum won't show up in your life fully formed. It's built, step by step, on the back of the small things that have the greatest impact.

IF IT'S THAT SIMPLE, WHY DON'T WE DO IT?

What stops us from starting small? Why is it that something as simple as making the bed or taking a ten-minute walk feels beneath us? The short answer boils down to three things: ego, fear, and perfectionism.

The ego wants us to look impressive from the outside. It wants to skip the warm-up and go straight to the highlight reel. Starting small doesn't build up our ego; it actually humbles it. And that's one reason many people avoid it. If the step isn't big, it must not count for anything of great significance. But that's a lie. The smallest steps are often the most strategic because they're the only ones we're likely to repeat.

Fear is another common trap. We fear failing, so we are slower to start. We fear being judged, so we wait for the day when everything is ready. But as you may have seen in your own life, fear's favorite phrase can become "maybe tomorrow." The longer we wait for the fear to subside, the harder it becomes to begin.

Perfectionism is another deterrent to our momentum. I know this one can get me from time to time. I overthink. I want everything dialed in before I start. But that mindset can create paralysis. If we decide we can't start with the smallest step until the conditions are perfect, we're killing our momentum.

I've always been a dreamer, a big thinker with an abundance mindset. But I've also learned that dreaming big doesn't work until we're willing to act small. Those big dreams only become a part of our reality when they're broken into small, repeatable actions. With an abundance mindset and a growth mentality, we can see challenges as opportunities and push forward even when our results are slow.

We can burn out when we start too fast without a solid foundation. It's like sprinting the first hundred yards of a marathon. We might feel powerful for a moment, but the crash is coming. We have to pace ourselves. Life is a marathon that requires our training.

When I was a teenager, we trained for a 50 mile walk with my church. We started the walk in the late afternoon, walked throughout the night, and finished the following morning. Many probably felt like me at first: "How hard can walking be? You just walk and don't stop."

Little did I know that a lot happens to your muscles as you walk that far without proper training and take small steps in preparation. Only a fraction of us were able to finish, and most of us who did had trained slowly and consistently by doing shorter walks that gave us the momentum to tackle the 50-miler in the weeks leading up to it.

> **Dreaming big doesn't work until we're willing to act small.**

So what about the person who finds themself in a pattern of repeated starting and stopping, who just can't seem to follow through? I don't think it's a discipline problem but instead a flaw in the design.

When our goals are too big or vague, they become overwhelming. Overload leads to inaction, and inaction kills momentum. The fix is to shrink the goal until it becomes unskippable. Create a system that works with your life, not against it. And give yourself the grace to start where you are.

We live in a culture addicted to instant results, quick fixes, and viral hacks. But anything meaningful takes time. The most important transformations come from progress over perfection. And the best momentum comes from motion rather than motivation.

Why?

Motivation is emotion-based. It's unpredictable. It's tied to a person's mood, the weather, or any other internal or external factors. But motion is action-based. It's controllable. You don't need to feel good to act; you just need to move. The first tiny motion bypasses the emotional resistance and creates the spark that motivation pretends to be. This is the basis behind Mel Robbins' book *The 5 Second Rule* and why it works.

Your behavior follows your belief.

When you're riding a bike from a dead stop, the first few pedals are the hardest. It's hard to start without standing up and really pushing down on the pedals to build speed. Once you build up speed, though, you can afford to coast. That is momentum. But if you stop pedaling, you run the risk of losing momentum and having to start again.

So the goal isn't to get motivated. It's to minimize friction and create tiny, repeatable motions that keep the wheels turning. Motion leads to momentum. Momentum creates progress. Progress builds motivation—not the other way around. Momentum isn't born in the mind; it's born in the motion.

Robbins says, "Confidence is built by the actions you take, not the thoughts you think."[65] James Clear echoes that idea when he says, "Every action you take is a vote for the type of person you want to become."[66]

Do you really want momentum in your life? Don't wait to feel ready or for perfect clarity. Start with what you can do right now. Let your small wins stack up, and let your systems or routines sustain you. Because the path to big change always starts with the smallest steps.

WE CAN'T DO IT ALONE

When I think back to the early years of my life, there's a clear thread that runs through every season of growth: I didn't get there alone.

We could do it alone, but it is a lot easier to get where we want to go with help. Someone has been there before and has the experience to assist you. It feels like asking for help will annoy people or make us seem weak, needy, or like we're imposing. But research and a whole lot of lived experience in my life tell a different story. When we ask for help, people are far more likely to say yes than we predict. Try it sometime.

A landmark study by Vanessa Bohns at Cornell University showed that people dramatically underestimate how likely others are to help them. On average, participants thought they'd need to ask twice as many people as they actually did to get help.[67]

Helpers reported feeling good about being asked, not burdened or annoyed. Asking for help doesn't make you weak; it makes you human. And humans build things together.

In Robert B. Cialdini's book *Influence: The Psychology of Persuasion,* he outlines reciprocity as one of the six core principles of persuasion. When someone does something for us, or even asks for our help, we feel a social obligation to respond. People don't like leaving debts unpaid, even emotional ones. Asking for help activates this natural inclination to give back.[68]

Whether it was football or baseball, my coaches had a significant impact on me. They didn't just run drills or yell from the sidelines; they helped me develop the skills that made me better. They pushed me when I wanted to coast. They corrected my form when I didn't even know it was off. That's the role of a great coach—they give you a perspective you don't usually see. And in life, we need the same thing.

As we get older, we start thinking we have to figure everything out on our own. But that's not how momentum works. Momentum is built in community with others. Life coaches, mentors, professional coaches, and even the right friends can all help accelerate our growth—not by doing the work for us but by helping us stay on track and encouraging us when we're tempted to quit. When we surround ourselves with the right people, their mindset, energy, and beliefs start to influence us. And sometimes that influence is exactly what we need to get ourselves unstuck.

Think about the saying *Show me your friends, and I'll show you your future*. That's not just feel-good advice; it's strategy. We rise or fall to the level of our environment, and who we spend our time with matters. If we want to become more disciplined, we need to spend time with disciplined people. If we want to think bigger, having coffee (or in my case hot chocolate) with people who live with an abundance mindset is a great way to spend a little time. Those kinds of examples will rub off on us.

I've found that even the smallest form of progress becomes contagious when we're in the right circles. Whether it's a workout partner who keeps us showing up, a business mentor who helps us map out our next steps, or a friend who challenges us to think deeper about our goals, those relationships are leverage. They're just what we need when we need to create lift in our lives.

Proximity is power, not because fulfillment automatically transfers by osmosis but because being around people who are pursuing growth reminds you that you can too. Their momentum creates space for yours.

Don't overlook the power in the seemingly simple act of creating your circle. Choose friends who build instead of break, invest in mentors, and seek out accountability. The people you run with shape the pace and direction of your race. And if you want to go far, it helps to go with the ones who've been where you're trying to go.

SHOW UP, ONE MICRO-GOAL AT A TIME

How do we build momentum when life feels anything but stable, when we're overwhelmed, underinspired, and unsure where to begin?

We start small—micro-small even.

If the last few years have taught us anything, it's that the human condition comes with no guarantee of certainty. Whether it's a personal crisis, a professional curveball, or a global disruption, life has a way of throwing things at us that we didn't ask for and can't control. But here's what we can control: our response, our next right step, and our internal circumstances.

That's why I keep coming back to micro-goals. They aren't shortcuts; they're strategies. They take something big and potentially overwhelming and make it doable. They lower the emotional barrier to starting. We don't have to move the mountain; we just have to pick up one pebble. When the road looks too long, a micro-goal can help us focus on the next 5 feet.

Small steps help keep overload at bay. They give us a place to begin. And when life gets shaky, having something small we can do helps stabilize our mindset and energy. We gain traction, which builds motivation, which builds belief. And that belief powers long-term change.

BJ Fogg breaks this down in his book *Tiny Habits*. His research shows that behavior change doesn't start with big promises or willpower. It starts with something so easy and repeatable that we can't fail. That's the brilliance of micro-goals. They're designed to succeed because they're achievable.

Fogg teaches that you don't build new habits by trying to overhaul your life overnight. You build them by anchoring small changes to things you already do. *After I brush my teeth, I'll do two pushups. After I make coffee, I'll write one sentence in my journal.* Over time, these small wins start to change your identity. You go from someone who tries to someone who does. When you celebrate each tiny win—whether it's two pushups or one sentence—you're reinforcing the behavior with positive emotion. And emotion is the glue that helps habits stick.

Now it's time for one of my favorite movie examples of all time: *Rudy*.

If you've never seen it, here's a quick setup. Daniel "Rudy" Ruettiger is a working-class kid who dreams of playing football at Notre Dame. He's too small, not extremely talented, and nobody expects him to make it. While watching a Notre Dame football game at home with his dad and brother on a little black and white TV, he announced to them that someday he would play football at Notre Dame. At that moment, not even his dad or his brother believed him. Unfortunately, in our lives, we are going to voice our dreams or aspirations, and we won't get the reaction we want. Don't let it hold you back. *Be a Rudy!*

He keeps showing up. Practice after practice, year after year. No fanfare, just grit. And that's where the magic is.

Rudy didn't earn his shot based on talent. He earned it through consistency. He built momentum by doing the small things right, again and again, even when no one was watching. That's what makes the movie so powerful. Whenever I need a little pep in my step, I listen to "The Final Game" from the movie soundtrack. You can't help but feel all the emotions Rudy felt when all his hard work paid off. In fact, as I write this, I am listening to the soundtrack.

One of the most pivotal scenes in the movie is Rudy's conversation with Fortune, the quiet and wise stadium groundskeeper. Rudy is beyond frustrated. He's been working for years, giving everything he's got, and he still hasn't made the list of players who got to dress for the game, making his chances of getting on the field impossible. He's finally ready to quit.

As Rudy walks through the tunnel, all packed up and about ready to quit on his dream, he finds Fortune on the field. And then Fortune speaks into his life with this truth:

In this lifetime, you don't have to prove nothin' to nobody except yourself. And after what you've gone through, if you haven't done that by now . . . it ain't gonna never happen.[69]

That moment flipped a switch for Rudy. Fortune helped him see that he was just wallowing in his own self-pity. He realized he wasn't doing it for the spotlight. He was doing it because he'd already proven something to himself. He'd become the kind of person who didn't quit. And in the process, he'd inspired a team of others to believe in him too.

That leads to one of the most emotional scenes in the movie. All the other players are bigger, stronger, and more gifted athletes than Rudy. And yet they walk into the coach's office one by one, place their jerseys on the desk, and say, "Coach, let Rudy play in my place."

That's what happens when you consistently show up, when you do the small things with excellence, even when no one else notices. You create a ripple effect. Others take notice. They're moved, and they show up for you too. At the end of the game in the movie when Rudy hasn't come onto the field yet, the whole stadium is chanting his name, "Rudy, Rudy." He looked up in the stands, and even his parents realized everyone was chanting his name. He had made an impact on so many. That moment wasn't just about football. It was about identity, support, and how much power we hold, not just in what we do but who we become by doing it.

There's another layer here that's easy to miss. Rudy could have walked past Fortune without ever speaking to him. Fortune was "just" a groundskeeper. But Rudy had the humility and curiosity to connect with him and listen. And that made all the difference.[70]

It's a reminder that your support system might come from unexpected places. But it starts with being honest. Express what you want, show up for the task, and share your wins with the people around you.

We talk a lot in our culture about self-made success. But no one truly makes it without others. Your environment, mentors, and friends all help shape who you become. Whether they lift you up or weigh you down, your circle matters.

If you're serious about building momentum, you also need to build a support system that reinforces the life you're trying to live.

Sometimes that support looks like a coach or mentor, someone who's been where you want to go and can help you see what you can't see. Sometimes it's a friend who reminds you who you are when you forget. Other times, it's the quiet voice of a groundskeeper telling you that you've already done enough. Support can also look like you being that voice for someone else.

So what's one micro-goal you can set this week?

Start simple. Don't overthink it. Read two pages of something inspirational each night before bed. Write down three things you're grateful for each morning. Stretch for five minutes while your coffee brews. Set a timer. Clean something for ten minutes and then stop.

None of these things sounds life-changing. But do them every day for a week and watch what happens. You'll start to feel more energized, focused, and grounded. You'll start to believe that change is possible because you have been proving it to yourself with each small action. And belief is the key that unlocks everything.

One of my favorite quotes, often attributed to Theodore Roosevelt, is this:

> It's not the critic who counts. . . . The credit belongs to the man who is actually in the arena . . . who strives valiantly . . . who, at the worst, if he fails, at least he fails while daring greatly.[71]

Get in the arena. Show up with one small act of courage at a time. When you do the smallest things with consistency, purpose, and heart, you'll have the opportunity to experience the greatest impact—not because they're impressive but because they build the kind of person who keeps showing up. That person already exists within you, and today is the perfect day to prove it.

Because what gets measured gets managed.

TAKE ACTION TODAY

In economics, opportunity cost is what you give up when you choose one option over another. So when you procrastinate, the opportunity cost isn't just the task you're delaying; it's everything you could have gained by doing it on time. For many, procrastination isn't about laziness; it's all about avoidance. It goes back to that four-letter word: FEAR. It is the fear of failure or imperfection.

I like the following harsh but true statement by Bishop Rosie O'Neal: "Procrastination is the arrogant assumption that God owes you another chance to do tomorrow what He gave you a chance to do today."[72]

Sustaining momentum requires support. That's why your next step includes both what you do and who you're doing life with.

We talked a lot about small wins and stacking micro-goals to get your momentum going. But let's take it a step further. If you want to keep your momentum going long after the motivation wears off, you'll need account-ability and encouragement. The right support system can become the fuel you need when your tank runs low.

In a world that constantly pushes us to go big or go home, the real wins actually come from going small and staying steady.

How do you build that kind of support? Start small.

Just like with your habits and routines, you don't need a massive mastermind group or a full-on personal board of directors right away. One or two trusted people who believe in your vision and are willing to hold you accountable are more than enough to begin. Whether a professional coach, a mentor who has been where you are, or a peer who shares your work ethic, just start with a conversation.

Others may seem like they're trying to hold you back. As Tony Robbins puts it, when you begin to grow or suc-ceed in an area, it can make others uncomfortable, not because you're doing something wrong but because you're holding up a mirror.[73] Your consistency becomes a quiet challenge to their complacency. And that's okay.

It's why discernment is just as important as discipline. We live in a time of unprecedented access to insight. With YouTube, podcasts, online courses, and even AI tools, we're flooded with opportunities to learn. What used to cost thousands of dollars and a plane ticket to a conference now lives in your phone. John Maxwell once shared how he bought a box of leadership tapes for around a thousand dollars early in his career. He and his wife sacrificed months of comfort so he could grow into who he felt called to be. Today, that same kind of material is free online, but the question becomes, *Will you use it?*

Live events like the ones I have attended by Brendon Burchard or Tony Robbins can electrify your sense of purpose in a way that solo study can't. There's something about being surrounded by people with similar energy and drive. That collective momentum is contagious. It reminds us that we're not alone. Yes, use the free stuff online. Explore and figure out who resonates with you. Then, when the time comes, step into the rooms where belief runs high.

Whether you start with a mentor on a screen or a friend at a coffee shop, what matters most is that you start. Build your support system one conversation at a time. Ask for feedback, invite accountability, and be someone who adds value, not just someone who receives it. As much as you need people in your corner, someone else might need you in theirs.

Start small and stay steady. One of the most powerful ways to generate momentum is to begin so small that failure isn't even an option. These micro-wins are easy to start, quick to execute, and deeply satisfying when completed. The trick is not to wait until you think you're ready but to start with what is right in front of you. These tiny acts might not seem life-changing on their own, but repeated daily, they set a tone of consistency and discipline. They help you reinforce the identity that you are someone who follows through.

To make these actions stick, anchor them to something you already do. These tiny triggers make your habits automatic. And when you track your progress, you give yourself visible proof that you're moving forward.

Celebrate your small wins. Check a box, say "yes" out loud, or high-five yourself. These little acknowledgments attach emotions to your progress, and that emotional reward is what makes lasting change. When in doubt, try the five-minute rule: If it will take you less than five minutes to complete, do it now.

Rewire your mindset. Sometimes the biggest obstacle to momentum is how we think. To reframe negative thought patterns, start by replacing "small" with "strategic." It's a simple shift that can change everything.

Silence perfectionism by reminding yourself daily that progress beats perfection every time. When fear creeps in, start by shrinking your goal. Make it skip-proof. Instead of launching an entire new routine, just observe yourself doing the first step.

Visualization isn't just woo-woo hype or an out-of-date technique from the Law of Attraction crowd. Done right, it's neuroscience meets performance hack meets momentum accelerator. And yes—it can be the difference between a goal you write down and a life you actually live.

Visualization builds the *identity* and *belief* that fuel the *behavior* that creates *momentum*.

It's like preloading your success so your actions are guided by clarity and conviction, not just discipline and grind. Your brain doesn't know the difference between vivid imagination and real experience—not in terms of neural activation. When you visualize yourself performing an action, your motor cortex lights up just as it would if you were actually doing it. This process strengthens neural pathways, which can improve confidence, readiness, and execution.[74]

One journal prompt you could ask yourself is this: *What small step feels beneath me but could build real momentum if I did it daily?* The resistance you feel toward a small task is a clue to where your next breakthrough might be hiding.

Build your support system. You don't need a twenty-person mastermind right now. You just need one or two people who will check in, cheer you on, and hold you accountable. Keep it casual but consistent. A weekly text exchange or short check-in can go a long way.

Success isn't just about talent; it's about relationships.

Build authentic, generous connections, and you'll always have people in your corner helping you move forward, even when your motivation fades. Keith Ferrazzi hammers this: Don't wait until you're stuck or lost to reach out. Build your network proactively. *Why?* Because when your emotional gas tank hits empty, you'll already have people ready to refuel you. Think of your network like a well—dig it when you don't need water yet. The bottom line in his book *Never Eat Alone* isn't just about networking; it's about designing your relational ecosystem so that even when your personal motivation is MIA, your support system steps in like a backup system to support you in sustaining your momentum.[75]

At the end of the day, you don't need more willpower; you need better relationships.

Reach out to someone you admire, whose character, energy, or expertise inspires you, and meet up with them. Ask questions and be curious. This kind of humble curiosity is what Rudy showed in his conversation with Fortune in the stadium tunnel. He didn't overlook the value of the person right in front of him, and it resulted in the opportunity to receive life-changing wisdom.

Finally, audit your circle. Ask yourself who builds you up and who drains your energy. Be intentional as you protect your environment. It's shaping you whether you realize it or not.

Design systems that stick. Goals get you started, but systems are what make your goal inevitable. Use a visual tracker to see your progress. Whatever keeps your wins visible will keep your energy high. At the end of each week, stack those wins.

Write down three things that worked and reflect on what made them successful. Then set a weekly system goal that is based on the process instead of an end result.

You're not trying to win the game in one move; you're building the conditions for long-term success. End each week by asking yourself what system would make your next step easier. The answer to that question will guide your next level of growth.

When you feel overwhelmed, return to the basics. Brain dump, reflect, and regroup. Celebrate the smallest win you can find and then build on it, because the habits you're creating now are the foundation of who you're becoming next.

Next, we'll talk about the habits of momentum that create movement and have the power to sustain it. Progress happens as we remain steady, so let's build habits to carry you forward, even when life gets messy.

CHAPTER 8

DEVELOP ROUTINES OF MOMENTUM

Have you ever had a day where you did everything right but still felt stuck? You woke up on time, crossed a few things off your list, and maybe even squeezed in a workout, and yet by dinner, it felt like momentum had somehow slipped through your fingers.

That used to happen to me a lot, and I couldn't figure out why. I'd blame my schedule, my willpower, or even just a bad mood. But the truth was simpler and even more frustrating. My habits were sabotaging my momentum, and I didn't even know it.

The funny thing is that momentum rarely disappears in one big moment. It leaks out slowly through small, unnoticed actions, not because we're lazy or broken but because our brains are efficient. And once the brain learns a loop, it just runs it automatically.

That's what makes understanding the difference between habits and routines so crucial. A lot of people use the words interchangeably, but they're not the same. They live in different parts of the brain. And more importantly, they serve different purposes when it comes to building momentum.

> **Momentum rarely disappears in one big moment.**

Habits are automatic. They live in the basal ganglia, the pattern-recognition section of the brain. They're built for energy efficiency. Once formed, they require little to no conscious thought. That's why we don't have to remind ourselves to brush our teeth or tie our shoes. We just do it. Habits are the brain's way of saying, "Let me save you the trouble of thinking."

Routines, on the other hand, are intentional. They require planning, focus, and effort. They live in the prefrontal cortex, the same part of our brain that handles willpower, decision-making, and long-term thinking. A routine is what you deliberately choose to do. It might include habits, but it also includes choices. That's what makes it powerful.

Here's how I think of it now: Habits run your life. Routines redirect it.

When we feel stuck, it's rarely because we don't know what to do. It's because we don't know what to do next. Ambiguity kills momentum faster than failure. That's why routines matter so much. A good routine doesn't just keep you busy; it keeps you aligned with who you're becoming.

And that's the key: *who you're becoming.*

So many people focus on what they want to have and then try to figure out what they need to do to get it. But that order is backward. Jim Fortin teaches it like this: be, do, have. First, decide who you want to be. Then take actions from that identity. And eventually you'll have the results that align with it.[76]

Ambiguity kills momentum faster than failure.

That's what routines can do. They aren't just boxes to check. They're tools to shape your identity. When your routines are anchored to identity, they last. Instead of relying on motivation, they run deeper.

Momentum isn't built in a day; it's built daily. And it loves rhythm. That's what led me to care more about continuity than perfection. What matters most is that I stay in motion, no matter how small the step. Because every time we follow through, we're casting a vote for the kind of person we want to become.

Charles Duhigg talks about keystone habits, small things that spark big change. They're like the lead domino. Push one, and a chain reaction begins.[77] For me, keystone habits have looked like journaling, stretching in the morning, and making my bed. They're not glamorous, but they remind me that I'm the kind of person who shows up, follows through, and builds momentum instead of waiting for it.

Our brains love momentum. They're wired for it. According to research, a huge percentage of our daily behavior is automatic. That means most of our lives are happening on autopilot because our brain is doing what it was designed to do: preserve energy.[78]

Momentum isn't built in a day; it's built daily.

So the question becomes this: What are we automating? In what direction is our autopilot pointing us?

When I started asking myself that question and answering honestly, I saw patterns I didn't like: mindless scrolling, late-night TV binges that stole my sleep and drained my energy for the next day. I used to say I needed those things to decompress. But what I really needed was a better default—something rooted in who I wanted to be.

The goal isn't to micromanage every moment. It's to design systems that move us forward even when motivation fades. Because it will. What we need isn't more hype; we need more rhythm, more structure, and more awareness of how our routines are either aligning us with our purpose or slowly pulling us away from it. Momentum is built by choice, not by accident.

WHEN TIME MANAGEMENT ISN'T WORKING

Why do so many of us double down on time management when we're already burned out? Because it feels like the only thing we can control.

Time is visible. We can measure it, block it, and color-code it. It feels tangible. But energy, on the other hand, is invisible. We can't see when our energy is leaking or when our emotional reserves are running low. We just feel off. And in a world that glorifies being busy, feeling off gets labeled as laziness, weakness, or lack of discipline.

So we tighten our calendars, stack more on our schedules, and convince ourselves that if we can just plan better, we'll get out of our ruts. We think things like this: "If I can put more on my calendar, I can dig myself out of this funk." It might work at first, but it's not sustainable. And we know it.

The problem is that most of us were raised to believe that success comes from grinding harder. Culturally, we hear things like "rise and grind," " sleep when you're dead," and "be the lion, not the gazelle." Productivity gets idolized. Busyness gets confused with progress. But we know that being busy doesn't always equal effectiveness.

Depending on your upbringing or the country you live in, your definition of success may be tied directly to how much you can do. And when doing more stops working, you feel like you're the problem—that you're failing or that something's broken in you. But that's not the truth. You're just out of rhythm.

Time management isn't a bad thing—it just isn't the *whole* thing. It doesn't account for what we're actually carrying. It doesn't factor in our emotional bandwidth or physical depletion. It doesn't recognize that our decisions are shaped by our energy.

With my work in sales, this is especially clear. If I'm not choosing the right activities, the needle doesn't move. And when my energy is off, it's much harder to make the right decisions. The human condition and life's circumstances will push us off track. And if all we're relying on is time management, we won't be able to sustain our momentum when that happens.

Time management isn't a matter of our minds; it's a matter of our hearts.

We don't need a better planner; we need a better rhythm. We don't need to do more; we need to feel differently. Until we shift the way we think about energy, we'll keep mistaking burnout for a motivation problem and solving the wrong thing.

CURATE YOUR ENERGY

I used to think I just needed more discipline. If I could just get more organized—wake up earlier, plan better, and work harder—I could finally get ahead. But what I've come to realize is this: We can have perfect time management and still feel stuck.

We need to focus less on what we do and more on how well we're able to show up for it—physically, mentally, and emotionally. And that's where energy management comes in. Time tells us when, and energy determines whether we have the capacity. We can schedule all the right things at all the right times, but if our energy level isn't there, those plans won't stick.

A 2012 study by Roy Baumeister on decision fatigue showed that willpower is a finite resource. The more energy we burn resisting distractions or temptations, the less we have left for the things that actually matter. In other words, energy shapes our decision quality. And when we manage our energy well, we replenish that willpower instead of constantly trying to muscle through exhaustion.[79]

It's why so many of us have tried to fix our lives by managing our time, only to find ourselves still overwhelmed or falling into self-sabotage. Time blocks don't override low energy. They don't bypass emotional fatigue. We can't journal our way out of burnout.

Momentum doesn't come from time; it's an energy phenomenon.

When we feel good physically, mentally, and emotionally, we naturally want to stay in motion. We make better choices. We stay focused longer, and we're more generous and present with people. Time management can't create that state, but energy alignment can.

> **Momentum doesn't come from time; it's an energy phenomenon.**

That's why I pay close attention to my rhythms. Most of the time, my energy is at its lowest in the afternoon—

especially after a big lunch—or later at night before bed. That's when I have to be the most careful, because unhealthy habits thrive in low-energy states, not because we're bad people but because we're depleted. And when we're depleted, we default.

We live in a world that sells energy in a can. Energy drinks are everywhere. They're marketed as solutions and quick fixes to help us push through. But most of them are loaded with caffeine, sugar, and hidden ingredients that create long-term dependency. Ask anyone who's tried to quit Diet Coke or cut back on coffee—it's not easy. That's because caffeine is a drug. And when we rely on it too heavily, we're not truly managing our energy. We're borrowing it, with interest. Real energy management comes from how we treat our minds and bodies.

And that starts with honoring the foundations of energy: sleep, movement, and nutrition.

One of the most important things we can do for our energy is get enough quality sleep. It isn't just rest. It's when our bodies restore physical energy and reset our mental and emotional systems. Sleep isn't a luxury; it's a non-negotiable.

So why do we need sleep? A full seven to eight hours of sleep matters because sleep isn't just one singular thing; it's a cycle. Throughout the night, your brain moves repeatedly through light sleep, deep sleep, and REM (rapid eye movement) sleep, each serving a different function. Early in the night, deep slow-wave sleep dominates. This is when the body does its heavy repair work: tissue repair, immune strengthening, growth hormone release, and metabolic regulation. The brain also clears metabolic waste through the glymphatic system, essentially taking out the neurological trash. Cut this short, and you wake up physically depleted even if you were unconscious for hours.

Later in the night, REM sleep becomes more prominent. This is when the brain integrates learning, consolidates memory, regulates emotion, and updates your sense of meaning and perspective. REM is critical for creativity, emotional resilience, motivation, and decision-making—the very traits people label as "discipline" or "drive." When sleep is shortened, REM is often the first casualty, which explains why chronic short sleepers may function but feel flat, irritable, or unmotivated. Getting seven to eight hours allows enough complete cycles for both body repair and mental integration. Momentum depends on energy, clarity, and emotional regulation—and sleep is the biological system that quietly underwrites all three. Strong days are built on complete nights.

Many cultures understand this. When I lived in Argentina, the siesta after lunch was normal. I used to think it was lazy, but now I realize it was smart energy management. When we get consistent rest, we think more clearly and bounce back faster.

My own energy dips in the early afternoon, which research suggests is typical, even after a full night's sleep. On days when my schedule allows, I close my office door, turn off the light, and take a fifteen-to-twenty-minute nap.

Those are the afternoons that I get a second wind and finish the day strong.

Throughout history, leaders and innovators have used napping as an energy tool. Leonardo da Vinci supposedly used a polyphasic sleep schedule, breaking his sleep into multiple naps throughout the day instead of one long period of sleep.[80] Thomas Edison power-napped,[81] and Churchill and Tesla[82] were both strategic nappers. Whether or not you nap, the principle holds: We don't build momentum by burning ourselves out. We build it by mastering the recharge cycle.

Movement isn't just for getting in shape or checking off an exercise goal for the day. It's one of the fastest ways to change our state. When we move, we increase oxygen flow to the brain, boost dopamine and serotonin, and signal to our body that it's time to wake up and engage with life. Even a short walk can reduce anxiety and increase dopamine.[83]

It doesn't have to be a grueling gym session. Some of my most productive days have started with nothing more than a brisk walk outside or a set of stretches between meetings.

If I hit a creative block, I've learned that pushing through at my desk rarely works. But stepping outside, moving my body, and letting my mind wander almost always does.

Like sleep, movement works in cycles. The more consistently you do it, the more energy you have to keep doing it. Momentum is built by giving your body the signal to move so your energy follows.

Nutrition matters more than we realize. The foods we eat directly affect our blood sugar, which affects our mood, focus, and energy levels. When our blood sugar spikes and crashes, so does our mental clarity. But when it's stable, we make better decisions, recover faster from stress, and sustain our energy throughout the day.

I've noticed that on days when I start with a healthier breakfast, I can avoid the mid-morning crash and think more clearly throughout the afternoon. And when I hydrate consistently, my energy stays steady instead of dipping into brain fog.

> **The trick is not to wait until you think you're ready but to start with what is right in front of you.**

Nutrition is a long game. We don't feel the effects of one meal forever, but we feel the compound effect of hundreds of choices over time. The more we treat food as a strategy for maintaining our energy instead of just a solution for our appetites, the more consistent our momentum becomes.

Most of us aren't taught how to manage our energy. We're taught to maximize our time. But time without energy is like having a car with an empty gas tank. It looks fine on the outside, but it's not going anywhere.

If you've been wondering why things haven't been sticking, it might not be a planning problem. It might be an energy problem. And that's something we can actually work with.

CREATE YOUR AUTOPILOT FOR MOMENTUM

Once we understand that most of what we do every day is not conscious but habitual and automatic, we'll stop chasing motivation and start designing systems or routines around the results we want.

Will Durant, in *The Story of Philosophy*, summarized one of Aristotle's ideas like this: "We are what we repeatedly do."[84] Neuroscience backs him up. In their diary study, Wood, Quinn, and Kashy found that habits in stable contexts are automatically triggered, meaning they require minimal conscious thought. Participants often thought of unrelated matters while acting on autopilot.[85]

In other words, the majority of our lives are being run by the part of our brains that is on autopilot. I bet that when you hop in your car, you usually end up at your destination without thinking about every minute of the trip.

Once we understand that most of what we do every day is not conscious but habitual and automatic, we'll stop chasing motivation and start designing systems or routines around the results we want.

That's why building momentum isn't about forcing willpower; it's about intentionally designing your autopilot. If a large portion of our days happens on autopilot anyway, why not make it work in your favor?

The good news is that even though most of our behavior is automatic, we can still make conscious choices to change our habits so they align with our goals and values. But here's the part you need to hear: There is no one-size-fits-all routine. The perfect morning routine you read about online might be a total mismatch for your life stage, your energy rhythms, or your responsibilities. The point is to create your own system, one you can maintain consistently and adjust when life changes.

If you've seen the movie *Groundhog Day*, you know the story of Phil, a news reporter stuck reliving the same day over and over. At first, he's annoyed, frustrated, and even angry when he wakes up and realizes it's the same day again. But over time, he starts to get creative. He learns piano, he learns to dance, and he improves himself. He uses each repeated day as an opportunity to build new habits and become a better version of himself.

What you're not changing, you're choosing.

To me, that's the ultimate metaphor for momentum and renewal. Sometimes life feels like we're stuck in a loop. All the days feel the same, and we're stuck in routines that aren't helping us grow. But what if we could use those loops to intentionally create positive habits?

Phil didn't get it right every day. Some days stunk. There were so many days when he stepped off the curb and into a pothole filled with icy water just to roll his eyes as he remembered it happening just like that the day before. But because he had the opportunity to try again, he started to see each day as a new chance to improve. Eventually, those small changes added up to a breakthrough. He changed his life and became a better person because of his choice to make changes. You have that same chance, even if it doesn't feel like it right now.[86]

A line I keep coming back to is this: *What you're not changing, you're choosing.*

If you want to lose weight but aren't changing your habits, you're choosing to stay the same. If you want to grow in your career but aren't doing anything besides complaining, you're choosing to stay miserable in your current place. Momentum doesn't happen by accident or by beating yourself up for what you haven't done. It happens when you make the small, consistent choices that will move the needle forward.

CREATE ROUTINES THAT WORK FOR YOU

A study analyzed roughly 12,000 workday diaries and found that small daily wins strongly predicted positive motivation, creativity, and engagement. In other words, we don't need to wait for massive breakthroughs to feel progress. Small wins compound into momentum.[87]

BJ Fogg's research at Stanford reinforces this. Behavior change doesn't come from bursts of motivation. It comes from small, consistent actions triggered by existing cues in our days. Want to start flossing? Pair it with brushing your teeth. Want to start doing pushups? Do them right after you make coffee.[88]

But I believe reflection is just as important as the habits themselves. Momentum needs fuel. And that fuel comes from recognizing progress. We can ask ourselves, *How does this routine connect to the life I say I want?*

If the answer feels emotionally strong, the habit becomes easier to stick to. In *Atomic Habits*, James Clear explains why routines tied to our identity stick more than those tied only to outcomes. He says, "Every action you take is a vote for the person you wish to become."[89] That's why our most important needle-moving activities need to be when we're at our best.

For me, that means making my most important calls between 9:00 and 11:00 each morning. That's when I have the energy and clarity to do my best work. You'll have your own peak performance window, and part of this process is to find it.

Researchers Lowenstein and Baumeister found that when energy is depleted, people misjudge their ability to take action. Energy loss skews perceptions, decision-making, and willpower. This is why we might have a great plan in the morning, but by 8:00 p.m., that plan is nowhere in sight, and there's a bowl of ice cream in our hand.[90]

Time management is linear, but energy management is dynamic. That means it's not enough to plan when we'll do things; we have to plan when we'll be at our best to do them.

Mornings matter. A morning routine matters because it works with your brain's biology instead of against it. In the first hours after waking, cortisol naturally rises as part of the circadian rhythm. Cortisol gets a bad reputation, but in the morning, it's useful. It increases alertness, focus, and readiness for action.

When you attach a consistent routine to this window, you're essentially harnessing a built-in energy surge and pointing it somewhere intentional. Add to that the fact that decision fatigue is lowest early in the day—your prefrontal cortex hasn't yet been worn down by choices—and you get a powerful combination: high energy, high clarity, and low resistance. That's fertile ground for momentum.

Morning routines also create what psychologists call behavioral priming. Repeating the same actions in the same order trains the brain to shift quickly into a productive state, reducing friction and reliance on willpower. Over time, this consistency reinforces identity ("This is who I am and how I start my day"), which strengthens follow-through across the rest of the day. Momentum thrives on predictability plus progress. A morning routine provides both predictability in structure and progress through early wins that signal to your brain, "We're moving." Once that signal fires, the day tends to organize itself around it.

For me, mornings are about setting the tone for the day. I avoid the news and social media first thing. If it's important enough, I'll hear about it. Most news is designed to be negative to keep our attention, and that's just not how I want to start my day.

Instead, I start with movement: exercise, yoga, or stretching, just to get my heart rate up. I hydrate immediately, aiming for about 20 ounces of water before coffee. Sometimes I add a pinch of salt or lemon juice for alkalinity.

If I have extra time, I'll use a sauna, especially in the winter months. Research shows sauna bathing boosts circulation, supports recovery, and triggers endorphins.[91]

Some people swear by cold plunges or showers. While I don't do this regularly, the science is compelling. Cold exposure increases alertness and focus, reduces inflammation, improves circulation, and can even build stress resilience.[92]

I also feed my mind with something positive, like an audiobook or podcast, on my morning walk. That way, my first mental inputs of the day are intentional instead of reactive.

End the day well. An evening routine matters because it regulates the systems that determine how well your brain and body recover. Sleep quality is one of the strongest predictors of cognitive performance, emotional regulation, and motivation, and it is heavily influenced by what happens in the hours before bed.

Consistent evening routines help synchronize the circadian rhythm by cueing melatonin release and lowering physiological arousal. Reducing light exposure, stimulation, and cognitive load at night allows the nervous system to shift from sympathetic "go mode" to parasympathetic recovery. When that shift happens reliably, sleep becomes deeper and more restorative, which directly fuels focus, discipline, and energy the next day—raw materials for momentum.

Evening routines also protect momentum by reducing mental residue. The brain is wired to seek closure; unfinished tasks and unresolved stress keep the mind in a low-grade state of alertness that fragments sleep and drains motivation. Simple practices like reflection, journaling, or planning tomorrow's top priorities help offload cognitive clutter and create psychological closure.

Evenings are meant to be about review and shutdown. This is where a lot of us can lose momentum. As the day goes on, discipline can crash. It's easy to binge TV, scroll endlessly, and sacrifice the sleep we need.

Decision fatigue can also play a role here. All day we've been making choices, and by evening, our willpower bank is empty. Low blood sugar makes it even harder to say no. That's why I created a shutdown sequence: lights off at a set time, read a few pages of a book, and have my phone on silent or in another room. I also reflect on the day, not to beat myself up but to consider what worked, what didn't, and what I can adjust for the next day. If I fall off track, I get back on quickly.

Reframe your evenings by focusing on alignment, not hustle. A simple wind-down ritual such as light reflection, planning one or two priorities for tomorrow, or disconnecting from stimulation creates a psychological runway. You wake up with direction instead of decision fatigue. That's huge. Momentum isn't built by heroic mornings alone; it's sustained by intentional endings. Strong days don't just begin well; they end well.

What we do before bed shapes our next day. Robert Stickgold supervised research on the Tetris effect, which shows that pre-sleep activities influence dreams and memory consolidation. Blue light from screens suppresses melatonin, while negative emotional input can bias our mood and energy for the next day.[93] Momentum isn't just about how forcefully you start; it's about how well you recover. An intentional evening routine ensures that each day ends cleanly so the next one starts with clarity instead of carryover.

Reflect on your routines. Momentum needs fuel, and one of the best fuels is intentional reflection. Too often, we get caught in a cycle of doing without pausing to ask ourselves if what we're doing is actually working. Reflection is the pause that keeps us from running on empty. It's a way to recalibrate, fine-tune, and make sure our energy is moving in the right direction.

> **The goal isn't to micromanage every moment. It's to design systems that move us forward even when motivation fades.**

Think of your routines like an autopilot system. It's useful when it's aligned with your goals, but it can drift if you never check the settings. Reflection is a time to ask if your routines serve your vision or if they're just something you've been doing out of habit.

Remember, when the *why* is emotional, the *how* becomes automatic. Even with a strong *why*, life changes. Priorities shift. Energy ebbs and flows. That's why reflection should become an ongoing practice.

Whether it's a weekly review, a quiet morning journal session, or a walk where you think about your progress, make reflection part of your rhythm. Momentum doesn't just happen; it's nurtured by awareness.

Decide what works for you. Everything I've shared about my routines works for me at the present, but it hasn't always looked like this. Your routines will change over time. Life seasons, family needs, career demands, and even your health will influence how you design your autopilot.

The key is to experiment. Try different approaches. Pay attention to how you feel, not just how productive you are. Keep the parts that give you energy and progress. Drop what doesn't fit.

And remember, momentum isn't built on perfection. Consistent, intentional effort that aligns with your natural rhythms and your deeper *why* will keep you moving in the right direction.

When you design your routines with purpose, you take the driver's seat back from those automatic habits that may no longer serve you. When your autopilot is reset toward your goals, momentum stops being something you chase; it becomes something you live every day.

Before you turn off the light tonight, ask yourself, *What's one small action I can take before bed to make tomorrow easier? Which habit feels like it's on autopi-*

lot, and is it taking me where I want to go? What's one piece of friction I can remove from my evening so I can actually rest?

When you wake up tomorrow morning, check in with yourself with the following questions: *How do I want to feel at noon today, and what can I do before 9:00 a.m. to make that happen? Which two actions will give me the most momentum before the world gets loud? If I do nothing else today, what's the one thing that will make me proud tonight?*

Find ways to shift your mindset from punishing yourself for what you haven't done to feeling excited about new possibilities. When you slip up, don't beat yourself up. Instead, give yourself grace. See setbacks as part of the process rather than an end. Treat each day as a new chance to get better, just like Phil learned to do in *Groundhog Day.*

There is no single perfect routine that fits all of us. What works for me might not work for you. The best momentum-building routines are those you create for yourself and can maintain and tweak as you grow.

Some days, you'll nail your routines—other days, not so much. That's okay. The point is to build an autopilot that feels doable, aligned with your energy and responsibilities, and flexible enough to adapt.

CHAPTER 9

CHOOSE MOMENTUM-BUILDING THOUGHT PATTERNS

This chapter is a tough one for me to write. There have been seasons in my life where my own mind feels like enemy territory. Thoughts circle in endless loops, whispering doubts, magnifying fears, and projecting worst-case scenarios that rarely come to pass. And yet my imagination is powerful enough to convince me they're already happening.

From years of studying personal development and researching human potential, I know the tools, techniques, and frameworks to help me with my thoughts. But I'm also human. I wake up each day and put my pants on one leg at a time, the same way everyone else does. You might assume that as the author of this book I'd have everything figured out—that I'm hitting the ground running, never losing momentum day after day; that I'm the epitome of all the best of what I've written for you.

Wrong.

As old as I am, I have certainly learned a lot. But I continue to learn. I keep allowing myself room to grow as I face life's challenges. I've come to see that everything we go through will teach us something if we're willing to look for the lesson. In that way, I feel like I'm walking alongside you, learning as we go.

So many of the personal development books I have read make me feel like the author has everything dialed in, like they transcended the struggle and didn't have to push themselves to get their momentum back. What I now understand is that this is rarely the case. We're all on different paths on this journey called life. Success isn't a single summit we reach; it's a winding path with serious peaks and valleys. It's a journey that is built over time and is very rarely a straight ascent.

This past year has been a tough one for me in a lot of ways. There have been moments when it has felt like everything around me was shifting and I didn't have much control over any of it. When we feel like life is happening to us instead of through us, it can shake our mental state, especially when we feel like we've been doing a pretty good job at living life.

Everyone wants to be in control. We want to be happy and successful. But as we've explored in other chapters, life's challenges can be self-imposed, or they can come out of nowhere and hit hard. Either way, there's no magic pill. We can't fast-forward through the hard parts. We have to live them out in real time and do our best to stay steady through them.

That's where hope comes in. When we lose hope, we're in trouble. Hope is the thin thread that connects our present struggle to a better future. It's the belief that "this too shall pass," even when we don't know how or when.

I'm not great at waiting for things to pass. I'm the kind of person who wants to fix things and fix them fast. Time's a-wasting, right? But some lessons only come with time, and some challenges simply cannot be muscled through. They have to be lived through.

It can feel like we're getting more than our fair share of tough times during different seasons of our lives. Each season is unique, with its own set of frustrations, fears, and unexpected turns.

Sitting here writing this, I wouldn't call myself the perfect example of positive thoughts and emotions. Most people who know me would probably describe me as upbeat, grounded, and steady. As my wife likes to joke, "Everyone loves Jeremy!"

Sometimes *Jeremy* doesn't really love Jeremy. Sometimes I don't feel like the best version of who I am or who I'm meant to be. Some days are better than others. Some days I show up and feel aligned, clear, and grateful. Other days it takes everything in me just to keep showing up.

And yet I do show up. That's the one thing I've learned to keep doing—showing up each day, even when I don't feel like it, and trying to learn from whatever the moment is teaching me. When something knocks me off course, I do my best to pivot, ask what the situation is trying to show me, and not let it keep me down for long.

Still, there are times when things don't unfold the way my mental vision has laid out. When that happens, my mind can build an entire alternate storyline out of those negative thoughts, like a movie reel that only plays tragedies. Every scene is dramatized and every outcome distorted.

That's the danger of unchecked thought patterns. They can turn our imagination into a weapon against ourselves. But that same imagination, when guided by awareness and intention, can also be our greatest ally. It can help us see beyond what's hard and reconnect us to what's possible.

We need to recognize when our minds start building stories that drain our energy and replace them with thought patterns that create momentum. We don't have it all figured out, and we don't have to pretend to.

RUMINATION AND SELF-PITY

We discussed rumination in an earlier chapter, but it deserves to be brought to your attention again. It's the tendency to replay events and imagine negative outcomes, or fall into those negative loops in our heads. Susan Nolen-Hoeksema, a researcher at the University of Michigan, found that rumination not only worsens depression but also prolongs the emotional distress of stressful life events. It fuels and prolongs negative moods, impairs problem-solving, and undermines social and emotional functioning. I think of it like watering weeds in the garden of your mind. The more attention you give them, the deeper their roots grow.[94]

Here's something to consider: You can't think two thoughts at once. Every time your mind replays a negative story, it's taking up space that could be used for something more positive and productive. I've learned the **Rumination can kill your momentum.** hard way that rumination can kill your momentum. It can feel like mental quicksand. The more we struggle with it, the deeper we sink.

Self-pity is often a form of rumination, and it tends to feed itself. What I have found is that rumination thrives in silence and stagnation, but momentum (action) kills it. Movement, conversation, or even humor can quickly short-circuit the self-pity spiral.

When something in life feels hard or unfair, I can slip into that *poor-me* mode. It feels supportive at first, like emotional comfort food. Self-pity strokes my ego while pretending to protect my heart. It tells me I'm the victim and that no one else understands how hard it is. It whispers, "You deserve a break. You've been through enough."

But self-pity steals our clarity, drains our energy, and robs us of being present and intentional about creating solutions. When we're in that self-pity loop, the spotlight is always on us. It helps us focus on our pain, disappointment, fear, and past mistakes. It narrows our lens so much that we stop seeing the people around us, their struggles, or their needs.

When we're stuck in self-pity, we aren't giving our best to anyone—not our spouse, our kids, our coworkers, or even ourselves. It's selfish, but it's also deeply human. And while it's tempting to beat ourselves up for being selfish, researchers like Nolen-Hoeksema have shown that self-pity and rumination are often default coping mechanisms when

> **Self-pity steals our clarity, drains our energy, and robs us of being present and intentional about creating solutions.**

people feel powerless.[95] So labeling it as selfish oversimplifies it. It's probably more accurate to say it's a protective response that has gone too far.

The real danger of self-pity is that it stalls momentum. It convinces us that we're the victims of our circumstances rather than being change agents. And ironically, the more we indulge it, the more isolated we feel. That isolation deepens the very loneliness and frustration we were trying to escape in the first place.

I have heard many times to "just think positive," and things will change. Positive thinking is important and has its place in gaining momentum, but to believe that simply thinking positive thoughts will change a circumstance is naive.

Thoughts don't float in a vacuum; they're shaped by biology, stress hormones, sleep debt, emotional load, and lived experience. When your nervous system is fried or your habits are misaligned, positive thinking can actually backfire. Psychology shows that forcing optimism during periods of stress can increase frustration and self-blame because you're essentially telling yourself you should feel better when your system clearly doesn't agree. That disconnect breeds guilt, not momentum.

What actually works is action before affirmation. Behavior changes biology faster than belief does. Small, concrete actions—movement, structure, reduced decision fatigue, finishing one manageable task—send signals to the brain that progress is happening. Those signals lower cortisol, restore a sense of agency, and then make more constructive thinking possible. In other words, you don't think your way into a better state; you act your way into one, and your thoughts follow. Positive thinking isn't useless; it's just a terrible starting point. Momentum doesn't begin in the mind alone; it begins when choices create evidence. And evidence, unlike wishful thinking, is something the brain actually believes.

Momentum isn't luck. It's a product of repeatable mental mechanics.

When I find myself going down that road, I've learned that I need to pivot—and fast. Because if I don't, my mind starts building entire storylines from that emotional fog, and before long, the narrative feels real. That's how powerful our thoughts are.

Our brains are naturally wired to spot problems. But what once protected us can now keep us stuck. Our modern

> **Time management is linear, but energy management is dynamic.**

environment rarely requires us to outrun a lion, but our brains still respond to everyday stress like we're under attack. The result is frustration, worry, and a constant scanning for what might go wrong next.

SHIFT THE SPIRALS

So how do we interrupt the cycle of negative thoughts?

One key is resilience, but not the kind we usually picture. We tend to think of it as bouncing back, like snapping a rubber band into its original shape. In reality, true resilience isn't about going back to the way things were. It's using setbacks as stepping stones instead of roadblocks and bouncing forward.

In her research on grit, Angela Duckworth found that passion plus persistence predicts success more reliably than IQ or talent. It's not the smartest or fastest who thrive long-term; it's the ones who keep going when things get hard. Resilient thought patterns don't deny reality; they reframe it. When something knocks you down, the resilient thinker asks, "What's the next step?" That one question keeps us in motion when others stay paralyzed.[96]

I call it the "Next Step Rule." Don't solve the whole problem or overthink the entire plan. Just decide on the next small step and take it. One small action interrupts the spiral of stuckness and reclaims your momentum.

Self-compassion is another incredibly powerful piece that I used to overlook. For a long time, I believed that being hard on myself kept me accountable. I thought if I could just push harder or expect more, I'd improve faster. But research by Kristin Neff, one of the leading voices on self-compassion, proves the opposite. Harsh self-criticism doesn't build momentum; it kills it.[97]

Having self-compassion means treating yourself with kindness when you fall short. And oddly enough, it actually increases motivation, because when failure isn't perceived as fatal, you're more willing to try again. Think about it: You wouldn't yell at your best friend and berate them when they make an honest mistake; you would offer your support and encourage them to keep going. So why not extend that same courtesy to yourself?

Being kind to yourself doesn't lower your standards; it raises your resilience. It changes "I really screwed up" to "I'm learning and improving every day." And as long as you're learning, you're still moving.

We need to remind ourselves that we're all human, we're all learning as we go, and we're all a work in progress. The next time you notice your critical thoughts starting up, ask yourself, "Is this what I would say to someone I care about in their time of need?" If the answer is no, rewrite the statement in a way that's firm but encouraging.

Over time, that practice retrains your inner voice and can become an ally instead of an enemy.

Once we learn how to pivot our thinking toward positivity, we begin to build the kind of thought patterns that sustain momentum for life.

MAKE SMALL ADJUSTMENTS THAT SHAPE THE WHOLE GAME

Momentum in life rarely comes from massive breakthroughs. It's built, preserved, and sometimes rediscovered through a series of small, intentional changes—tiny adjustments that seem insignificant in the moment but compound into something powerful over time.

We often expect transformation to arrive like a lightning strike, but it's more like a quiet shift. Life is like golf in that way. The difference between a slice and a straight shot might be as simple as where the ball sits in your stance or how you hold the club face on the backswing. Just a few degrees off, and you can spend the rest of the hole chasing the correction. Yet when you make that small adjustment, everything falls into place again.

The same is true with how we think. Our thoughts are often the swing mechanics of our lives. Those repeated patterns determine where the ball ultimately lands. And while we can't control every bounce, we *can* learn to approach each shot, each day, and each moment with a bit more awareness and grace.

Golf has always fascinated me because it's such a game of precision and patience. Every element matters. And yet when something goes wrong, the fix is rarely dramatic. I often think about how the better you get at golf, the more you can feel where you went wrong. A new golfer who doesn't have the practice or tools will often get frustrated and say things like, "I have no idea what I am doing wrong." That is why many quit the game. They didn't put in the time and practice to be able to know what led to the results. The best players don't panic; they make a small tweak. They check their alignment, breathe, refocus, and try again.

In life, we often expect something big—a new job, a new relationship, a new year—to fix what feels off. We love the idea of new beginnings because they hold hope. But as I've learned, new beginnings don't erase what came before; they build on it. Just as in golf, each hole contributes to your overall score. You can't pretend the first few didn't happen, but you can adjust your mindset for the next one.

That's where small changes matter most. When we step back and recognize that momentum isn't about avoiding mistakes but about staying in motion *through* them, we start to play the long game of life differently—a small shift in how we think about a setback, a brief pause before reacting, or the decision to speak to ourselves with grace rather than criticism. These small, often unseen adjustments become the difference between a life that spirals out of frustration and one that continually recenters on growth.

I've always loved new beginnings. Each one offers a fresh sense of possibility and a clean scorecard for the day ahead. But I've realized there's a subtle trap in constantly chasing the new.

If we tell ourselves that everything starts over each time the calendar flips, we might forget that life is cumulative. Our habits, thoughts, and choices build on each other. The results we see today are the outcome of thousands of small decisions we've made before.

That doesn't mean we're stuck with past mistakes; it just means that lasting change is more about integration than reinvention. Shaka Senghor went to prison as a nineteen-year-old for second-degree murder and ultimately spent the next nineteen years incarcerated. What makes his story remarkable (and uncomfortable) is what happened inside prison. He taught himself to read and write, discovered philosophy and literature, and began a long, brutal process of personal responsibility rather than self-justification. He doesn't minimize what he did, and that's part of why people listen to him.

After his release, Senghor became a bestselling author of *Writing My Wrongs* and *Letters to the Sons of Society*. He has been featured on major podcasts (Tim Ferriss, Rich Roll, Brené Brown) and now speaks on accountability, justice reform, and personal transformation. His core message isn't redemption as a fairy tale; it's reckoning, ownership, and change through sustained action.

There's something powerful about acknowledging that our progress is an accumulation of moments, not the erasure of them. It's the willingness to learn from our mistakes, make the adjustments, and go back out there again that defines real momentum.

So much of what disrupts our progress doesn't come from external challenges; it comes from the voice inside our own head. Negative self-talk can be subtle, almost unnoticeable, but capable of setting everything off-course. We tell ourselves we're not good enough, replay past failures in slow motion, or create stories about what others think of us.

And before long, those thoughts start to shape not only our performance but our health, our relationships, and our sense of peace.

I've been thinking a lot about this lately, how our thoughts create pathways in the brain that reinforce themselves over time. Neuroscientist Norman Doidge wrote a book called *The Brain That Changes Itself*, explaining how repeated thoughts rewire our neural pathways in a process called neuroplasticity. What that means in simple terms is that the more we think a certain way, the more automatic that thought pattern becomes.[98]

In other words, neuroplasticity is our brain's momentum engine. It is our brain's ability to rewire itself based on repeated thoughts, emotions, and actions. It is what allows habits to form, skills to sharpen, and unfortunately negative patterns to dig deep grooves too. Think of it like wet cement on your mental infrastructure. Every thought and behavior we repeat carves a pathway. Once the cement dries on a specific pathway, your brain defaults to it automatically, like cruise control for your mindset. This is why we must be careful with our thoughts.

Neuroplasticity doesn't care whether your repetition is positive or destructive. It's neutral. It just obeys whatever you feed it. Every thought is like a vote for a future neural pattern. So if you are not intentional, you end up reinforcing the very circuits that make you feel stuck. Momentum isn't just about motion. It's about direction and consistency.

If you spend your days rehearsing self-doubt, your brain gets better at producing it. If you spend time practicing gratitude or compassion, your brain starts to favor those instead.

It's not just philosophy; it's physiology. And that's what makes awareness so important.

We can't simply "think positive" and expect everything to change overnight. That's not how the mind works. In fact, as Mel Robbins pointed out on her podcast, trying to fight negative thoughts with positive ones often backfires because it adds another layer of pressure, leaving us asking ourselves, "Why can't I just be positive?" Instead, the key is learning to redirect, to engage your mind in something new rather than battling what's already there.[99]

On the golf course, if you hit a bad shot, you can't just tell yourself, "Think positive." You have to take action on a strategic adjustment. You might check your alignment, change your grip, or adjust your mental focus for the next swing.

The same is true with our thoughts. When we notice negative patterns like fear, comparison, and self-criticism, the goal isn't to deny them but to reengage our mind elsewhere. Go for a walk. Do something creative. Talk to someone who lifts you up. Change the channel instead of arguing with the static.

That small redirection can reset your momentum faster than any forced positivity. Over time, these intentional shifts train the brain to naturally move toward healthier thought patterns, just as a golfer's muscle memory improves with practice.

That's the real work of sustaining momentum: shortening the distance between discouragement and recovery.

Life will always have its rough patches. Even the pros can lose their swing for a season. I remember hearing about Ian Baker-Finch, a golfer who won the Master's Tournament green jacket in 1991, one of the highest honors in the sport, and later walked away from it all because he couldn't find his rhythm again. He lost his swing, and no amount of effort could bring it back. What makes his story so haunting is that this wasn't a physical breakdown; it was a mental collapse under pressure. He tried for years to fix it—coaches, swing changes, restarts. Nothing stuck.

Eventually, he couldn't even put the ball in play in competition and retired from professional golf in his early thirties. That's almost unheard of. He later reinvented himself as one of the most respected broadcasters in golf, but as a player, his game never came back.

That story reminds me of how fragile confidence can be. Momentum, like a golf swing, is a delicate balance between form and freedom. Push too hard, and you tighten up. Get careless, and you lose control.

But the lesson here isn't about perfection; it's about staying curious. When things start to feel off, instead of judging yourself, what if you asked, "What small adjustment do I need right now?" Maybe it's rest. Maybe it's discipline. Maybe it's simply grace. Because sometimes what we need most isn't a complete restart but a recalibration.

That theme comes to life in the movie *The Senior*, a story about a fifty-nine-year-old man who goes back to finish his senior year of college football. He's carrying decades of regret, pain, and unfinished dreams, shaped by a complicated relationship with his father. And yet despite all the reasons not to, he decides to go back and try again.

In an interview on the Covenant Eyes Podcast, Mike Flynt explained that after high school, he received a full football scholarship to Sul Ross State University. He was an all-conference linebacker with a ton of accolades and became the team captain as a senior.

He got into a physical altercation with a freshman who wasn't following curfew, which led to Mike being removed from the team. He had to leave the college within an hour of being told the news. When his dad started to let him know what he thought about the situation, Mike replied, "Daddy, I am exactly what you made me." And the two of them never talked about it again.

He transferred to the University of Texas where he met the woman he married. After becoming a strength and conditioning coach, he maintained his own physical fitness by developing a philosophy of never asking his athletes to do something he couldn't do himself.

But getting kicked off his team all those years ago was the biggest regret of his life. When he learned that he still had a semester of eligibility, he felt physically ready to try out. He wanted to be part of the team and be there for the current team as a way to make up for the players he let down all those years ago. He got to pass insight on to his teammates, who looked up his history at their school and had questions.[100]

The movie isn't really about football; it's about redemption. It's about realizing that it's never too late to step back onto the field, even if you know you won't win. What matters is showing up differently this time—with humility, perspective, and a new understanding of what success really means.

We all have versions of ourselves that we'd like to go back and redeem. But we can't relive the past; we can only bring what we've learned into the next moment. That's what growth looks like: not a rewrite, but a renewal.

One of the most important lessons I've learned is to give myself grace. We can be so harsh with ourselves when things don't go perfectly. The problem isn't the bad day itself; it's how long we let it define us. When we start to believe that one bad day means we're bad at the game of life, we lose perspective. But when we remind ourselves that every time something doesn't go as planned it's actually part of a larger journey, we reclaim our sense of agency.

Momentum isn't lost in a single mistake; it's lost when we stop believing the next step matters. So instead of spiraling into self-criticism, what if we said, "That's okay. Let's adjust. Let's learn. Let's keep going." Grace doesn't excuse a lack of effort. It sustains effort when the results don't show up immediately. It gives us the space to breathe, course-correct, and keep showing up even when the scorecard isn't pretty.

LITTLE WINS, BIG IMPACT

When I think about momentum now, I see it less as a wave to catch and more as a rhythm to cultivate. It's found in the accumulation of little wins—the moments we choose to stay consistent, the thoughts we redirect, the adjustments we make quietly in the background.

The key is to honor the compounding power of small shifts over time. That's how neuroplasticity works. That's how mastery works. That's how a person turns a pattern of self-doubt into one of self-trust.

We don't need to overhaul our lives to change direction. If we can learn to see growth as an ongoing, forgiving process, then no matter what happens, we'll always be in motion because life is about alignment. And that's something we can adjust every single day.

Every thought you have is either serving your momentum or slowing it down. And because every person's brain is wired differently, shaped by their experiences, stresses, and stories, there isn't one perfect strategy that works for everyone. The goal isn't to find *the* method; it's to experiment until you find *your* method. That's what this chapter is really about—awareness, experimentation, and small, repeatable actions that keep you moving forward when your thoughts want to hold you back.

Experiment and adjust. Think of this section as a training ground. Just like the golf course, you don't master your swing overnight. You practice, test, and adjust. The same applies to your thought life. Some tools will click instantly; others will feel awkward at first. That's normal. The point isn't perfection; it's curiosity. You're not trying to fix your brain; you're learning how it works.

Our brains love evidence. Once we believe something, we start collecting proof to support it. That's why negative thought loops can become so powerful. Each time we replay a moment of failure, our mind stores it as confirmation. The more we repeat that loop, the more our brain believes it's true.

But the opposite is also true. When we start to intentionally feed our minds with new evidence, like examples of progress, gratitude, resilience, and growth, we can rewire the pattern.

That's what experimentation is for. Not everything will stick, but something will. And once you find what works, you can use it again and again to stay grounded in the middle of life's noise.

Recognize and redirect. The most powerful moment in any thought spiral is the first moment you notice it. The simple act of catching yourself in the middle of a negative loop immediately reduces its power. That's because awareness turns what felt like inevitability into a choice.

Mindfulness research confirms this. When you recognize a thought as just a thought, not an absolute truth, your brain's emotional response softens. You create a small gap, and that gap is where change happens.

> **That's the danger of unchecked thought patterns. They can turn our imagination into a weapon against ourselves.**

Once you've noticed the pattern, the next move is redirection. Don't overcomplicate it. You're not trying to force a positive thought. You're simply shifting your focus to something constructive, something that builds rather than breaks your energy.

Here's a simple framework you can practice: Notice the trigger ("I just told myself I can't handle this"). Label it ("That's a self-doubt thought"). Reframe it ("This is training; I'm learning how to handle more").

Cognitive therapy research shows that when you change the meaning of a thought, you also change your emotional and behavioral response to it. Over time, these small reframes compound into new automatic habits of thought, a mental muscle memory that supports your momentum instead of sabotaging it.

Choose your driver. Every morning, there are two drivers waiting in your mind. One fuels doubt, fear, and worry. The other fuels focus, gratitude, and determination. The question is, which one gets the keys?

Elite athletes know this well. They use deliberate self-talk and visualization to prime their focus before they ever step onto the field. They don't wait for the game to start to get in the right mindset; they choose their driver before the race even begins.

You can do the same. Before your day starts, decide who's driving your mind.

If the wrong driver takes the wheel, take the keys back. Redirect, adjust, and start again. Momentum doesn't come from having perfect days. It comes from training yourself to reclaim control when your mind tries to steer off course.

Move your body and engage your mind. When you get stuck in your head, one of the best things you can do is move. Go for a walk. Work out. Do something physical that reconnects you to your body.

I like to go for walks while listening to podcasts or audiobooks that feed my mind with positivity and growth. Sometimes I do chores or small tasks around the house while playing something that shifts my focus from worry to possibility.

The reason this works is simple. The body anchors the mind. When your thoughts are spinning, movement brings you back to presence. You're signaling to your brain, *I'm here; I'm safe, and I'm engaged.*

These small resets don't just clear your head; they build resilience. They teach you that no matter how loud your thoughts get, you can always choose to move toward better alignment.

Practice gratitude. When rumination or self-pity creeps in, gratitude is one of the most powerful counter-forces. You can't stay in self-pity and gratitude at the same time. They can't coexist.

Self-pity turns the camera inward; gratitude turns it outward. It shifts attention from what's missing to what's already present, from scarcity to abundance.

When I feel negativity starting to build during my morning routine, I become intentional about my breathing and begin listing what I'm grateful for, sometimes out loud. Even something as simple as "I have another day to grow and serve" can change my energy.

Researchers Robert Emmons and Michael McCullough found that gratitude journaling not only boosts mood but also improves physical health. Gratitude literally rewires your attention system, training your brain to look for good instead of danger.[101]

Here's a simple practice: Each morning, write down three specific things you're grateful for. At night, note one small win, no matter how minor. Over time, your brain starts scanning for evidence of progress. And that's what keeps momentum alive—emotional traction.

Serve someone else. Rumination is like a selfie; it keeps the lens focused inward. Service flips the camera around. When you serve others, you interrupt the feedback loop of negativity and turn your attention toward purpose. You replace powerlessness with contribution. It doesn't have to be dramatic. In fact, the smaller the act, the better.

Send one encouraging text every day. Offer your skill or expertise to someone who needs it. Do one unexpected act of kindness for your spouse, partner, or child. Volunteer at your church, a local food pantry, or a community project.

Service builds emotional momentum because it reconnects you to meaning. You realize that your life can have an impact, even on a bad day. That simple truth can reset your perspective faster than any motivational quote.

Rumination robs us in solitude. Human connection reminds you that you're not alone. Serving others increases dopamine and serotonin, the brain's feel-good chemicals, while reducing symptoms of depression and anxiety. But more than that, it helps you remember you're part of something bigger.

Reframe and replace. If you want to build lasting momentum, start by listing your most common self-sabotaging thoughts. Write them out. Don't judge them; just notice them. Then for each one, write a simple alternative framing.

For example, "I'm failing" becomes "I'm learning." "I can't handle this" can be "This is training." Or "I'll never get there" can shift to "I'm on my way."

Each time you catch one of these thoughts during your day, practice the reframe. The more you do it, the faster it becomes instinctive. Today's intentional reframe is tomorrow's reflex.

Positive psychology shows that optimism and reframing not only improve emotional well-being but also increase problem-solving and goal achievement. We have the power to choose interpretations that empower you instead of drain you.

Become, then do, then have. Most people operate the opposite way. They think, "If I have X, then I can do Y, and then I'll be Z." For example, "If I have enough money, then I can hire a trainer, and then I'll be fit." Or "If I have more confidence, then I can start that business, and then I'll be successful."

Real transformation doesn't start with what you have; it starts with who you are. You don't wait until life hands you the right circumstances to take action. You begin by deciding who you must be. Then you take action from that identity. When your being and doing align, the results naturally follow.

It's not about forcing yourself to grind harder or chase bigger goals. It's about anchoring your actions in identity. Because when your identity changes, your behaviors follow. When your behaviors follow, your outcomes change. Identity drives action, and action drives results. That's the leverage point most people miss.

This transition from being to doing isn't always clean or quick. Identity shifts take time. You don't flip a switch and instantly become a new person. It's more like strengthening a muscle—you practice, you stumble, you recalibrate, and then one day you realize you're living in alignment with the kind of person you decided to be.

Earlier in the book, I shared a quote by Jim Fortin, "Information without transformation is just entertainment."[102] It's a reminder that learning, reading, and even listening to podcasts or books—none of it matters if it doesn't change who you're becoming. Knowledge without identity change just stays on the surface.

One small action interrupts the spiral of stuckness and reclaims your momentum.

That's why mindset work matters so much. You can set all the goals in the world, but if you still see yourself as someone who can't follow through or someone who's always falling short, your results will keep reflecting that identity. On the other hand, when you start saying, "I am the kind of person who shows up" or "I am the kind of person who finds a way," everything you do starts to match that belief.

It's *be, do, have*—not *have, do, be*. Decide your identity before creating the action. Focus on your character before the outcome. When your momentum grows from who you are, not just what you do, it lasts.

Plan for the storms. The worst time to learn to sail is in the middle of a storm. Yet that is how most people live. They only start practicing emotional regulation, discipline, or mindset work when they're already in crisis. The truth is that storms aren't an *if;* they are *when*. Preparation isn't pessimism; it's wisdom. Anchors aren't meant to keep us from moving forward; they keep us from drifting too far when the waves get rough. They can give us stability while we adjust the sails. Let's look at the different kinds of anchors we can gather before the storm hits.

Values anchor us, so know your non-negotiables. If we don't know what we stand for, the storms will decide for us. Routines can help us build habits that ground us when everything around us feels chaotic. Know your support system so you don't have to wait until you are drowning to know who to call for help. Practice strengthening your power of perspective with reframing and being able to interpret challenges through a growth lens when they hit. Save, skill up, and diversify so you are ready to pivot if the financial need arises.

Nothing is worse than being limited by a lack of resources because you weren't prepared. And probably the most important one in my mind is having a spiritual anchor. This is your ballast. When the seas test you, you need something greater than logic to hold onto.

As Viktor Frankl said in *Man's Search for Meaning,* even in the worst conditions imaginable, we still have one last human freedom: the ability to choose our thoughts.[103] That choice determines the quality of our life, regardless of circumstance.

You can't always choose the course, but you can always choose how you play it.

Keep practicing. Momentum isn't built once; it's maintained daily. Every time you notice a thought and redirect it, you're strengthening your mental muscle. Every time you choose gratitude over complaint, you're aligning your mindset. Every time you serve someone else, you're adding fuel to your purpose.

Over time, these small repetitions become your new normal.

Rome wasn't built in a day, but it was built brick by brick, so keep stacking your bricks. The storm isn't the time to build walls; it's the time to trust that the walls will protect you. In other words, momentum isn't built in the storm. It's revealed by what you practiced before it.

SUSTAIN YOUR GROWTH, DEFINE YOUR LEGACY

As I write this final chapter and think about what I want to leave you with, my mind keeps going back to a simple phrase I've heard many times: "Being broke is hard. Becoming wealthy is hard. Choose your hard."

Momentum isn't about chasing the easy path, because there really isn't one. The results of staying stuck are hard. So is growing. Both require something of us. The difference is that one moves our life forward, and the other keeps us cycling through the same patterns. That's why we need to remember that we always have the oppor-

> **Momentum isn't just about motion. It's about direction and consistency.**

tunity to choose our hard. It's tied to another truth that can be uncomfortable to admit: We're choosing everything we aren't changing.

I've talked a lot about grace and self-understanding. I know momentum is influenced by our choices, but it's also influenced by the circumstances that blindside us and shape us in ways we didn't ask for. I understand that deeply, but the whole point of this book is in the title, *Own Your Momentum.*

Every transformation begins with personal accountability for both where we are right now and the direction we're heading.

At some point, each of us has to decide we are responsible for our lives. Nobody else can do the work for us or want it more than we do. Every transformation begins with personal accountability for both where we are right now and the direction we're heading.

A lot of my mindset comes from growing up with coaches who believed in high standards. I played sports throughout my college years, and my coaches were both encouraging and demanding. They expected results, and because of that, we practiced again and again so we were prepared at game time.

I wish I had gotten to know my grandfather, Leonard Johnson. I'm sure he would have had a lot to teach me as I grew up, but unfortunately he died from leukemia when

I was very young, so I don't remember him. I only have stories. He was a school principal and high school football coach in Preston, Idaho, and I was always told his players felt like the games were easy because his practices were so difficult. Coaches like him see your potential and then push you toward it. He pushed his players hard—not to break them but to prepare them—so when it came time for game day, they were ready.

That's the role I hope this book has played for you—supportive, of course, but also challenging you to rise to what you're really capable of. No more excuses or hiding out in the someday category. The time to change your life is now.

INSIGHTS TO KEEP IN MIND

Excuses are momentum killers. They're sneaky because they make us feel like we're protecting ourselves. When we have an excuse, it feels like the problem is out of our hands, so we can sit back and stay comfortable with the way things are. But every time we justify why we're not moving forward, we trade growth for the illusion of safety.

Excuses are momentum killers

The victim mindset works the same way. It convinces us that life is happening *to* us rather than *through* us. But momentum only becomes real when we accept responsibility for our direction. The moment we stop blaming circumstances, people, and timing is the moment we take our power back. When we drop the excuses, we become the author of our own story, and that's when our momentum begins to accelerate.

Be careful with comparison. Sometimes seeing someone else succeed can push us in the right way, but more often it has the opposite effect. It can make us feel small. It makes us forget that social media only shows the highlight reels over the hard times. Nobody gets to decide that we are less-than or somehow unworthy.

Almost two decades ago, when I was thinking about switching companies, I went to my boss to let him know. He responded by saying I should get a job with a salary because this business wasn't for me. In that moment, I decided to use his words as motivation. I didn't argue or fight back. I just quietly decided that my results would tell the story. Since then I've spent most of my mortgage career in the top 1 percent of originators in the country—not because I'm special but because I refused to let someone else's opinion become my identity.

Understand the importance of visualization and manifestation. When we picture a better future, we're not pretending our past didn't happen. We're simply refusing to let it define us. The brain doesn't fully distinguish between imagination and real experiences, so when we see ourselves succeeding, we're preparing our body and mind for those moments.

Research done by neuroscientists found that the experiences we visualize or imagine work in the same way as our real experiences. "[Our research] suggests that imagination is not passive; rather, it can actively shape what we expect and what we choose."[104] Momentum feeds on movement, and movement only requires direction instead of perfection. When we take the time to visualize who we are becoming and stay aware of where we've been, we bring our full story into the process.

Don't misunderstand what dreaming is. I've often been called a dreamer, and not always in a positive way. The dream isn't the shortcut; it's the blueprint. The bridge between a dream and reality is work. We can't just make ourselves busy and expect our dream to come to fruition. We have to be focused, intentional, and purposeful with our efforts. When fear or doubt shows up, the only way through is action—not sitting around and thinking about it or researching forever, but doing the thing that actually moves us forward.

> **The dream isn't the shortcut; it's the blueprint.**

Learn to be a dreamer who is also a realist. One of my sons loved basketball and wanted to become a professional player. He even dressed up as LeBron James one year for Halloween. We didn't want to crush that dream. Over time, he matured, evaluated his chances honestly, and let those dreams evolve. He still dreams, just in new directions that align with who he is and his strengths.

That's what I want for all of us. We should dream, but we should also be real. Not everyone is going to be the best in the world at something, but we can all become the best versions of ourselves. Most people live far below their potential because they let fear or doubt convince them they are limited in some way. But I'm living proof that our potential is greater than we realize.

Don't downplay the simple path to success. In my life, I've never met a successful person who didn't out-work the people around them. Sometimes it really is that simple. Work harder, want it more, stay consistent, and keep an abundance mindset. There is room for everyone to succeed. Scarcity is a mindset that steals momentum because it convinces us that someone else's win is our loss, and that is never true. Your biggest competition is your complacency, not another person who is out there creating forward motion for themselves.

CURATE YOUR BELIEFS, INTENTIONS, AND ENVIRONMENT

> **Momentum isn't lost in a single mistake; it's lost when we stop believing the next step matters.**

You picked up this book because you want to grow, influence others, and make an impact. That starts with becoming your best self so you can share that light with people around you. Let's dive into the three things that can sustain your long-term momentum.

Before any goal can take shape, you have to believe you are capable of change. You are your greatest asset. At the very least, you can believe your life has meaning because you were created with worth that is fixed and unconditional. When I was young, I was told, "You are a child of God, and God doesn't make junk." And if that's true, then you already have more potential than you may realize. Belief also naturally supports hope. When you believe in yourself, you open the door to hope for a better future.

Intention comes next. Casualness brings casualties. We can't drift our way into momentum. We have to be intentional about what we want and how we move toward it. Intentions can be powerful, but without taking initiative, we aren't going anywhere. Brendon Burchard says, "It's always a great day to grow."[105] As long as we're taking action, even when we fail, when we get back up and learn from it, we'll succeed. Momentum requires purposeful routines, clear goals, honest self-reflection, and choosing actions that serve instead of sabotage us.

Last but not least is your environment. Momentum thrives or dies based on the environments we place ourselves in. That includes the people we spend time with and the thoughts we entertain daily. A cluttered mental environment slows everything down. The people around us will either lift or lower our standards. That's why we need to be aware and choose wisely.

FINAL THOUGHTS

Challenges will still come. Hard seasons will show up throughout your life. But instead of asking "Why me?" ask, "What can I learn from this?" Whether the situation is your doing or completely outside your control, there is always something to take from it that will make you stronger or more prepared to help someone else later.

If you have a dream, go for it. Jump. If you never do, you stay exactly where you are, and you'll never get an answer to "What if?" I don't want to live a life full of what-ifs. I don't want to look back and wonder who I could have become.

For most of my life, I've dreamed of flying. I've even had recurring dreams of it, which is pretty comical considering the fact that I don't like heights. My favorite superhero growing up was Superman. My wife knew this, and for my thirtieth and fortieth birthdays, she bought me sky-diving tickets. At first, I said no way. The fear was *loud*. I tried my best to talk myself out of it.

But the more I sat with it, the more I knew I had to try. I didn't want fear to make my decisions for me. And I also remembered the person jumping with me had hundreds of hours of experience. Sometimes in life we need to lean on the experience of others to take the next step.

I did jump twice and loved it so much each time that I wanted to get back on the plane and do it all over again. Sometimes the exhilaration and sense of accomplishment come after doing the hard thing that we didn't want to do or thought we couldn't do.

Without goals, we drift. People without goals end up working for people with goals. That sounds harsh, but it's often true. So take the time to get clear. What do you want? What can you learn?

Without goals, we drift.

What experiences do you want to have? Write down fifty things—not just bucket-list items but real personal goals. When you have that clarity, your mind begins to filter the world differently. The reticular activating system in the brain helps us notice what aligns with our goals.[106] Our brain will start to work for us instead of against us. We'll see opportunities we used to miss. We'll say yes to things that move us forward and no to things that drain us.

Momentum is built on clarity, belief, action, and consistency. It's sustained by choosing your hard, taking responsibility, dreaming and working intentionally, and refusing to let fear or comparison dictate your potential.

Here is my final question for you: *How wonderful do you want your life to be?*

I can only share what I've learned and some tools that have worked for me. Now it's up to you to take what works for you and keep moving forward toward your relentless dream. It's up to you to create your own wonderful life. You have what it takes. You always have.

Now go out there and own your momentum.

ACKNOWLEDGMENTS

I want to thank all those family members and friends who listened to my personal story and my ideas and thoughts as I put together the chapters of this book.

I also want to thank Sarah and Tracy for their guidance and support throughout this journey of bringing this project to life.

ABOUT THE AUTHOR

Jeremy Johnson is a student of human behavior and a guide for people who know they're capable of more but feel stuck getting there. With a degree in psychology and decades of experience in performance-driven work, he has spent his career studying what creates momentum—and what quietly stalls it.

He is a VP, Sales Manager, and mortgage loan originator based in Fairfax, Virginia, ranking in the top 1% of mortgage originators in the country. Through his own seasons of doubt, pressure, and reinvention, Jeremy discovered that momentum—not motivation—is the true driver of lasting change. His work blends practical psychology with real-world experience to help people silence self-doubt, break limiting patterns, and take intentional action toward meaningful growth.

He lives in Virginia with his wife and three sons, who are navigating their own paths to create lives of impact.

Contact Jeremy at:

ownyourmomentum@outlook.com

NOTES

1 Dale Carnegie, *How to Stop Worrying and Start Living: Time-Tested Methods for Conquering Worry* (New York: Simon & Schuster, 1948), 22.

2 Brené Brown, *I Thought It Was Just Me: Women Reclaiming Power and Courage in a Culture of Shame* (New York: Gotham Books, 2007).

3 Orison Swett Marden, The Paralysis of Fear (Kessinger's Legacy Reprints, 2010, originally published in the early 1900s).

4 Jon Acuff, *Soundtracks: The Surprising Solution to Overthinking* (New York: Baker Books, 2021).

5 James Clear, *Atomic Habits: An Easy & Proven Way to Build Good Habits & Break Bad Ones* (New York: Avery, 2018), 27.

6 Mihaly Csikszentmihalyi, *Flow: The Psychology of Optimal Experience* (New York: Harper & Row, 1990).

7 *Atomic Habits,* 157.

8 *Pursuit of Happyness,* directed by Gabriele Muccino (Culver City, CA: Columbia Pictures, 2006).

9 Jennifer L. Taitz, *Stress Resets: How to Soothe Your Body and Mind in Minutes* (New York: Hachette Go, 2024), ix.

10 Roy F. Baumeister, *Meanings of Life* (New York: Oxford University Press, 2002), 5.

11 *Stress Resets*, xvi.

12 *Stress Resets*, xvi.

13 Robert Greene, *The Laws of Human Nature* (New York: Viking, 2018).

14 Bessel van der Kolk, *The Body Keeps the Score: Brain, Mind, and Body in the Healing of Trauma* (New York:

Viking, 2014).

15 Erwin Raphael McManus, The Last Arrow: Save Nothing for the Next Life (New York: Waterbrook, 2011).

16 *Atomic Habits,* 29.

17 *For Love of the Game*, directed by Sam Raimi (Burbank, CA: Universal Pictures, 1999).

18 Linda Stone, "Screen Apnea: What Happens to Our Breath when We Type, Tap, Scroll," *The New York Times*, August 21, 2023.

19 Andrew Huberman, "The Fastest Way to Reduce Stress in Real Time," YouTube, 3:09, October 18, 2024, https://www.youtube.com/watch?v=mPpB6Df3qQk.

20 *Atomic Habits,* 60.

21 Anna Lembke, *Dopamine Nation: Finding Balance in the Age of Indulgence* (New York: Dutton, 2021).

22 Eckhart Tolle. *The Power of Now: A Guide to Spiritual Enlightenment* (Novato, CA: New World Library, 1999).

23 Cal Newport, *Digital Minimalism: Choosing a Focused Life in a Noisy World* (New York: Portfolio, 2019).

24 Jana Meier, et al., "Distinct Trajectories of Perceived Control over Aversive Stimulation Predict Affective Reactions to Stressors Over and Above Objective Control," *Scientific Reports* 15, no. 1 (October 7, 2025).

25 Sadeghi, Ramin, Naghmeh Mokhber, Leili Zarif Mahmoudi, Negar Asgharipour, and Hamid Seyfi, 2015. "A Systematic Review and Meta-Analysis on Controlled Treatment Trials of Metacognitive Therapy for Anxiety Disorders." *Journal of Research in Medical Sciences* 20 (9): 901–909. PMC4696377. https://pmc.ncbi.nlm.nih.gov/articles/PMC4696377/

26 Maureen Salamon, "Doomscrolling Dangers," *Harvard Health*, September 1, 2024, https://www.health.harvard.edu/mind-and-mood/doomscrolling-dangers.

27 Anna Katharina Schaffner, "Understanding the Circles of Control, Influence & Concern," *Positive Psychology*, June 21, 2023, positivepsychology.com/circles-of-influence/.

28 Suzy Welch, "The Rule of 10-10-10," Oprah.com, September 1, 2006, https://www.oprah.com/spirit/suzy-welchs-rule-of-10-10-10-decision-making-guide.

29 "The Rule of 10-10-10."

30 Hall, Alena. "Survey Explores Generational Differences in Attitudes Toward Mental Health," *Forbes*, June 24, 2024. https://www.forbes.com/health/mind/generational-attitudes-mental-health-survey/

31 Grant Benham, "Bedtime Repetitive Negative Thinking Moderates the Relationship Between Psychological Stress and Insomnia," *Stress & Health* 37, no. 5 (2021): 949–61, https://doi.org/10.1002/smi.3055.

32 Lucas S. LaFreniere and Michelle G. Newman, "Exposing Worry's Deceit: Percentage of Untrue Worries in Generalized Anxiety Disorder Treatment," *Behavior Therapy* 51, no. 3 (2019): 413–23, https://doi.org/10.1016/j.beth.2019.07.003.

33 Judith S. Beck, *Cognitive Behavior Therapy: Basics and Beyond*, 2nd ed. (New York: Guilford Press, 2011).

34 Lauren E. Sherman, et al., "The Power of the Like in Adolescence: Effects of Peer Influence on Neural and Behavioral Responses to Social Media," *Psychological Science* 27, no. 7 (2016): 1027–35, https://doi.org/10.1177/0956797616645673.

35 Judson Brewer, *The Craving Mind: From Cigarettes to Smartphones to Love – Why We Get Hooked and How We Can Break Bad Habits* (New Haven: Yale University Press, 2017).

36 BJ Fogg, *Tiny Habits: The Small Changes That Change Everything* (Boston: Houghton Mifflin Harcourt, 2019).

37 *Atomic Habits*, 38.

38 Angela Duckworth, *Grit: The Power of Passion and Perseverance* (New York: Scribner, 2016).

39 Viktor E. Frankl, *Man's Search for Meaning* (Boston: Beacon Press, 2006), 97.

40 Roy G. Baumeister and John Tierney, *Willpower: Rediscovering the Greatest Human Strength* (New York: Penguin Books, 2012).

41 Kalina Christoff, et al., "Mind-Wandering as Spontaneous Thought: A Dynamic Framework," *Nature Reviews Neuroscience* 17, no. 11 (2016): 718–31.

42 J. Paul Hamilton, et al., "Default-Mode and Task-Positive Network Activity in Major Depressive Disorder: Implications for Adaptive and Maladaptive Rumination," *Biological Psychiatry* 70, no. 4 (2011): 327–33.

43 Marcus E. Raichle, "The Brain's Default Mode Network," *Annual Review of Neuroscience* 38 (2015): 433–47.

44 *The Legend of Bagger Vance*, directed by Robert Redford (Los Angeles: 20th Century Fox, 2000).

45 Jim Loehr and Tony Schwartz, *The Power of Full Engagement: Managing Energy, Not Time, Is the Key to High Performance and Personal Renewal* (New York: Free Press, 2003).

46 *Atomic Habits,* 27.

47 Mel Robbins, *The 5 Second Rule: Transform Your Life, Work, and Confidence with Everyday Courage* (New York: Savio Republic, 2017).

48 Jill Bolte Taylor, *My Stroke of Insight: A Brain Scientist's Personal Journey* (New York: Viking, 2008).

49 Judson Brewer, M.D., *Unwinding Anxiety: New Science Shows How to Break the Cycles of Worry and Fear to Heal Your Mind* (New York: Avery, 2021)

50 Paul Tassi, "The World's Best 'Clash Royale' Player Has Spent $12K on the Game, and for Good Reason," *Forbes*, April 1, 2016, https://www.forbes.com/sites/insertcoin/2016/04/01/the-worlds-best-clash-royaleplayer-has-spent-12k-on-the-game-and-for-goodreason/.

51 James E. Loehr and Tony Schwartz, *The Power of Full Engagement* (New York: Free Press, 2003).

52 Robbins, Tony. "Private Efforts, Bring Public Triumph." YouTube Shorts, 0:00. Posted by Tony Robbins, January 21, 2025. https://www.youtube.com/shorts/WpAuZxCiPbE

53 Steven Furtick, *Crash the Chatterbox: Hearing God's Voice Above All Others* (Colorado Springs: Multnomah Books, 2014), 181.

54 "What the Baader-Meinhof Phenomenon Is and Why You May See It Again . . . and Again," *Healthline,* accessed February 18, 2026, https://www.healthline. com/health/baader-mein-hof-phenomenon; Joseph H. Arguinchona and Prasanna Tadi, "Neuroanatomy, Reticular Activating System," StatPearls, accessed February 18, 2026, https://www.ncbi.nlm.nih.gov/books/NBK549835/.

55 Brian Tracy, *Success Is a Journey: Make Your Life a Grand Adventure* (Provo, UT: Executive Excellence Publishing, 1999), 11.

56 Bessie Anderson Stanley, "Success," *Your Daily Poem,* accessed February 18, 2026, https://www.yourdailypoem.com/list-poem.jsp?poem_id=2394.

57 *Peaceful Warrior*, directed by Victor Salva (Santa Monica, CA: Lionsgate, 2006).

58 Harvey Mackay, foreword to Brian Tracy, *Success Is a Journey: Make Your Life a Grand Adventure* (Provo, UT: Executive Excellence Publishing, 1999), 8.

59 Sharon Lebell and Epictetus, *Summary of the Art of Living: The Classical Manual on Virtue, Happiness and Effectiveness—A New Interpretation by Sharon Lebell* by Epictetus (San Francisco: HarperOne,2013), 15.

60 Thomas Jefferson, "Thomas Jefferson Encyclopedia," The Jefferson Monticello, accessed February 18, 2026, https://www.monticello.org/encyclopedia/if-you-wantsome-thing-you-have-never-had-spurious-quotation.

61 "Admiral McRaven Addresses the University of Texas at Austin Class of 2014," YouTube, 19:36, posted by "The University of Texas at Austin," May 20, 2014, https://www.youtube.com/watch?v=yaQZFhrW0fU.

62 Admiral William H. McRaven, *Make Your Bed: Little Things That Can Change Your Life . . . and Maybe the World* (New York: Grand Central Publishing, 2017).

63 Dave Ramsey, *The Ramsey Show* (Ramsey Network, Nashville, TN), radio program, https://www.ramseysolutions.com/shows/the-ramsey-show.

64 *Tiny Habits*, 30.

65 Mel Robbins. "A Toolkit for Confidence: How to Build UNSHAK-ABLE Self Confidence." YouTube, March 6, 2023, https://www.youtube.com/watch?v=kMtNkJcJn3M.

66 James Clear, Atomic Habits, 38.

67 Vanessa K. Bohns, "Underestimating Our Influence over Others' Willingness to Help," Cornell University ILR School, 2014, accessed December 11, 2025. https://ecommons.cornell.edu/entities/publication/9570112c-6c4e-4cc5-8021-a2ab530a143b

68 Robert B. Cialdini, *Influence: The Psychology of Persuasion,* rev. ed. (New York: Harper Business, 2006).

69 *Rudy*, directed by David Anspaugh (Culver City, CA: TriStar Pictures, 1993).

70 *Rudy*.

71 Theodore Roosevelt, "Citizenship in a Republic," speech, Sorbonne, Paris, April 23, 1910.

72 Bishop Rosie O'Neal, X (formerly Twitter), October 10, 2018, 11:18 a.m., https://x.com/BishopRosie/status/1050057902042562564.

73 Tony Robbins, "This Is the #1 Thing Preventing People from Achieving Success," *The Rubin Report*, January 1, 2025. https://www.youtube.com/watch?v=bsi45Kya8wg.

74 "The Power of Visualization: Imagining Yourself Doing Something Helps You Achieve Your Goal," Rowan Center for Behavioral Medicine, July 2, 2025, https://rowancenterla.com/the-power-of-visualizationimagining-yourself-doing-something-helps-youachieve-your-goal/.

75 Keith Ferrazzi, *Never Eat Alone: And Other Secrets to Success, One Relationship at a Time* (New York: Currency, 2005).

76 Jim J. Fortin. "Honestly, You Can Be, Do and Have Everything You Want When…" *The Jim Fortin Podcast*, episode 235, September 14, 2022. https://www.jimfortin.com/episode-235-honestly-you-can-be-doand-have-everything-you-want-when/.

77 Charles Duhigg, *The Power of Habit: Why We Do What We Do in Life and Business* (New York: Random House, 2012).

78 Wendy Wood, Jeffrey M. Quinn, and Deborah A. Kashy, "Habits in Everyday Life: Thought, Emotion, and Action," *Journal of Personality and Social Psychology* 83, no. 6 (2002): 1281–97.

79 Mark Muraven and Roy F. Baumeister, "Self-Regulation and Depletion of Limited Resources: Does Self-Control Resemble a Muscle?" *Psychological Bulletin* 126, no. 2 (2000): 247–59.

80 Walter Isaacson, *Leonardo da Vinci* (New York: Simon & Schuster, 2017).

81 Nancy F. Koehn, *Forged in Crisis: The Power of Courageous Leadership in Turbulent Times* (New York: Scribner, 2017).

82 Matthew Walker, *Why We Sleep: Unlocking the Power of Sleep and Dreams* (New York: Scribner, 2017).

83 John J. Ratey and Erik Hagerman, *Spark: The Revolutionary New Science of Exercise and the Brain* (New York: Little, Brown, 2008).

84 Will Durant, *The Story of Philosophy* (New York: Simon & Schuster, 1926), 87.

85 Wood, W., Quinn, J. M., & Kashy, D. A. (2002). Habits in everyday life: Thought, emotion, and action. *Journal of Personality and Social Psychology*, 83(6), 1281–1297. https://doi.org/10.1037/0022-3514.83.6.1281

86 *Groundhog Day*, directed by Harold Ramis (1993; Burbank, CA: Columbia Pictures).

87 Teresa Amabile and Steven Kramer, *The Progress Principle: Using Small Wins to Ignite Joy, Engagement, and Creativity at Work* (Boston: Harvard BusinessReview Press, 2011).

88 *Tiny Habits*, 40.

89 *Atomic Habits,* 38.

90 George Loewenstein and Roy Baumeister, "The Effects of Resource Depletion on Decision Making," in *A Handbook of Process Tracing Methods for Decision Research,* eds. Michel Schulte Mccklenbeck, Andreas Kuehberger, and Rob Ranyard (New York: Psychology Press, 2011), 279–92.

91 Tanjaniina Laukkanen, et al.,"Association Between Sauna Bathing and Fatal Cardiovascular and All-Cause Mortality Events," *JAMA Internal Medicine* 175, no. 4 (2015). 542–48.

92 Susanna Søberg, et al., "Thermal Stress and Cold Exposure: Effects on Alertness, Inflammation, and Metabolism," *Cell Metabolism* 32, no. 12 (2020): 1–15.

93 Erin J. Wamsley, et al., "The Tetris Effect: Prior Task Exposure Influences Dreams," *Cognitive Brain Research* 22, no. 1 (2004): 132–5.

94 Susan Nolen-Hoeksema, "The Role of Rumination in Depressive Disorders and Mixed Anxiety/Depressive Symptoms," *Journal of Abnormal Psychology* 109, no. 3 (2000): 504–11.

95 Susan Nolen-Hoeksema, Blair E. Wisco, and Sonja Lyubomirsky, "Rethinking Rumination," *Perspectives on Psychological Science* 3, no. 5 (2008): 400-24, https://pubmed.ncbi.nlm.nih.gov/26158958/.

96 Angela Duckworth, *Grit: The Power of Passion and Perseverance* (New York: Scribner, 2016).

97 Kristin Neff, *Self-Compassion: The Proven Power of Being Kind to Yourself* (New York: William Morrow, 2011).

98 Norman Doidge, M.D., *The Brain That Changes Itself: Stories of Personal Triumph from the Frontiers of Brain Science* (New York: Penguin Books, 2007).

99 "How to Stop Negative Thoughts & Reset Your Mind for Positive Thinking," The Mel Robbins Podcast, May 7, 2025, https://podcasts.apple.com/us/podcast/how-to-stop-negative-thoughts-reset-your-mind-for-positive/id1646101002?i=1000706676722.

100 Mike Flynt, *The Senior: My Life As a 59-Year-Old College Football Linebacker* (Nashville: Thomas Nelson, 2009).

101 Robert A. Emmons and Michael E. McCullough, "Counting Blessings Versus Burdens: An Experimental Investigation of Gratitude and Subjective Well-Being in Daily Life," *Personality and Social Psychology* 84, no. 2 (2003): 377–89.

102 Jim Fortin, "Episode 8: 'Reprogramming Your Subconscious Mind for Health, Wealth and Happiness,'" The Jim Fortin Podcast, April 10, 2019, https://www.jimfortin.com/reprogramming-your-subconscious-mind/.

103 Viktor E. Frankl, *Man's Search for Meaning* (Boston: Beacon Press, 2006), 65.

104 Lisa Marshall, "Your Brain on Imagination: Study Reveals How the Mind's Eye Helps Us Learn and Change," *CU Boulder Today*, December 10, 2025, https://www.colorado.edu/today/2025/12/10/yourbrain-imagination-study-reveals-how-minds-eye-helps-us-learn-and-change.

105 Brendon Burchard, "Daily Fire: It's a Great Day to Grow," *The Brendon Show*, podcast audio.

106 Daniel J. Siegel, *Mindsight: The New Science of Personal Transformation* (New York: Bantam Books, 2010), 39–45.